THE COMPLETE GUIDE TO

LUMBER YARDS AND HOME CENTERS

Other books by Gary D. Branson

The Complete Guide to Barrier-Free Housing: Convenient Living for the Elderly and the Physically Handicapped

The Complete Guide to Recycling at Home: How to Take Responsibility, Save Money, and Protect the Environment

The Complete Guide to Remodeling Your Basement: How to Create New Living Space the Professional Way

THE COMPLETE GUIDE TO

LUMBER YARDS AND HOME CENTERS

A Consumer's Guide to Choosing and Using Building Materials and Tools

GARY D. BRANSON

BETTERWAY PUBLICATIONS, INC.
WHITE HALL, VIRGINIA

Published by Betterway Publications, Inc.
P.O. Box 219
Crozet, VA 22932
(804) 823-5661

Cover design by Rick Britton
Cover photograph courtesy of Ace Hardware Corporation.
Typography by Park Lane Associates

Library of Congress Cataloging-in-Publication Data

Branson, Gary D.
      The complete guide to lumber yards & home centers : a consumer's
    guide to choosing and using building materials and tools / Gary
    Branson.
          p. cm.
          Includes index.
          ISBN 1-55870-209-1 (pbk.) : $14.95
          1. Workshops--Equipment and supplies.   I. Title.
    TT152.B76 1991
    690--dc20   91-19204
                                                                  CIP

Printed in the United States of America
0 9 8 7 6 5 4 3 2 1

Dedicated to Laura and John Branson

Acknowledgments

I would like to thank all the manufacturers who provided artwork and photographs.

Contents

Introduction

The first twenty-five years of my working life I spent as a contractor, involved in various phases of home building. A major part of my building education involved learning to sort out which building products were superior in terms of both applicability and performance in service. As most consumers have learned, there is a vast difference in quality among products offered in the marketplace. As an old tutor once told me, some products are made to serve, and some are made to sell.

In mid-career I began to write how-to articles and books for the do-it-yourself homeowner, then took a job as technical editor of a magazine called *The Family Handyman*. Through the years I've been writing I have tried to supply my readers with the best possible instructions for accomplishing a given task, and to improve on limited product label advice by offering insights I've gained from my own hands-on experience. At some point I came to the realization that much available how-to information is sorely lacking in at least one important area: how to make the necessary buying decisions when selecting building materials and tools.

Many sources of how-to information, such as magazines, are dependent on advertising income for their existence. It would be highly imprudent for the magazine writer to bite the hand that feeds him by suggesting a favorite among the many products available. That is the reason that many magazine articles have a "buyers' guide," listing every known product manufacturer at the end of each feature. It is done to avoid offending any current or potential advertiser. The same is true of TV how-to shows that depend on sponsor dollars: one either mentions the sponsor's product or none at all.

The professional construction journeyman has an advantage over the do-it-yourselfer: if the pro has trouble with a particular material that he is using, he can search out a different, more suitable brand of material for the next job. For the do-it-yourselfer, there often is no next job, because many amateur projects are undertaken on a once-in-a-lifetime basis. Thus the homeowner cannot employ the pro's trial-and-error approach to product selection. And if the amateur selects an inferior product or material, he may complicate the job, he may greatly increase the degree of difficulty of the labor to do the job, and he will probably end up with inferior results in spite of his extra efforts.

I can recite one excellent example of this hard-to-come-by buying knowledge. Back in the '60s I worked with a number of painting contractors. As anyone who has a house with painted siding will know, painting over chalking or oxidized paint is a difficult job, and the results are often less than satisfactory. Paint simply will not adhere well to a poor base such as chalking paint.

The pros tried every possible remedy to overcome the problem of chalking paint. We sanded, scrubbed, and scraped the old paint surface to clean it; we used oil-base primer as a means of locking down the paint particles and providing a base that would support a new paint film. Most often the result was premature paint failure and peeling due to poor adhesion of the new paint.

Then a new latex paint became available, heavily promoted for its ability to cover over failing paint coats. If you are old enough you may remember the TV and print ads for Olympic Overcoat paint. An old-timer who appeared to be a prospector came riding his horse onto the TV screen. He then extolled the ability of Overcoat to "cover old paint." His horse bolted at this announcement, and the old-timer tried to calm him: "Not you, Old Paint: that old paint!" he said, gesturing toward the ranch house.

The pros quickly tried this new acrylic latex paint and were pleased by the results. Soon every painter I knew was using Olympic Overcoat for covering difficult surfaces such as chalked paint, as well as using it as a premium-quality paint for new work.

In addition to improved paint formulas, new cleaners for use in cleaning decks and other exterior surfaces have been developed, and some cleaners also do a good job of cleaning away the chalking paint, so it is no longer a barrier to a lasting paint job. The point is that not only are latex exterior paints such as Olympic Overcoat and Benjamin Moore highly ranked (by Consumers Union tests) for use over chalking paint surfaces, but that one can now clean away the chalking paint before painting, using wood cleaning products in conjunction with pressure washers. Obviously, if the paint surface is clean one can choose any paint desired as a topcoat. Yet more than twenty-five years later, many consumer paint guides still advise us to use only alkyd (oil) paint to cover chalked paint surfaces. This advice is outdated, and it also is a problem for those who are environmentally biased toward using water-base paints. The consumer requires more product knowledge to enable him to choose the right product for the job.

The second drawback to doing home projects yourself is a lack of proper tools. When using the wrong tool, some jobs merely become time-consuming and difficult. But many jobs are impossible unless you have the tools for the trade. For example, the retaining nuts on a kitchen faucet are usually located between the sink back and the sink bowl, as seen from the underside. A special extension wrench, called a basin wrench because its design lets you reach into this difficult cavity alongside the sink basin, will help you remove and replace your sink faucet. In this confined space, if you try to use just any wrench you happen to have handy, you will quickly become frustrated with the task and may give up on what is really a fairly simple job—if you use the right tool.

One other observation: many how-to instructions attempt to help but give bad advice. For example, for painting wide drop siding on a house, one may be tempted to suggest a 4-inch-wide brush. Now that is good advice for those who have arms like a blacksmith. But if you are small, or elderly, or simply don't have the arm strength to swing a loaded 4-inch brush all day, there is simply no good reason you should not drop down to a smaller brush size, down to a 3-inch or even a 2-inch brush. You'll work more comfortably and get more done if you select a tool you can handle.

The same is true for power tools: I have a contractor's model circular saw, and I wouldn't trade it for a farm in Texas. It has power to spare and will stand up to continuous use. But it is one heavy brute, and for the occasional user or for a smaller person, the saw is definitely overkill. There are plenty of circular saws that will do the job without the extra weight. You should always check a tool for weight, balance, and ease of handling before buying it.

In this book we will attempt to guide you through buying decisions for the tools and materials you'll need to keep the homestead in shape. In most cases it pays to buy quality goods. Beyond that, there are two tips to keep in mind:

If you find a good product, buy a lifetime supply because they will quit making it next week.

And: You don't always get what you pay for, but you never get more than you pay for.

1.
Tools

An old adage in the building business states: "By the tools you will know the workman." For the pro, it's always smart to buy the best tools available. While quality tools are a definite plus for the homeowner, in some instances buying pro-quality tools may be overkill. For example, if you are not a dedicated do-it-yourselfer, you might buy a "good" electric drill for occasional and light duty, rather than paying the price for the "best" drill that is intended for daily or heavy-duty use by a pro.

For hand tools, however, quality is essential even for tools that will see only occasional use. The reason is that, in buying hand tools, cost savings between cheap and quality tools are small, at most. Buying a cheap hammer, for example, might save a couple of dollars. It also might mean buying a hammer whose head could chip, with possible injury to the user from flying steel. The blade of a cheap saw may bend and the teeth become dull if the blade is of inferior steel. Chisels must have sufficient steel quality so the blades will take and hold a sharp cutting edge. Give some thought to tools as you purchase them. Will the drill be used to build a house, or will it see occasional use for pre-drilling screw holes in plaster?

BUYING A BASIC TOOL KIT

While a basic tool kit can come in handy, even for the apartment dweller, a tool kit is mandatory equipment for the homeowner. A basic kit might include a small *carpenter's claw hammer*, perhaps a 14-oz. finishing hammer. This will let you do minor projects such as installing drapery hardware or putting new weatherstripping around a door.

Buy a small pair of *pliers with wire-cutting jaws*. This plier can be used for small gripping jobs and for cutting picture wire. Also for gripping and tightening loose nuts, buy a *6-inch adjustable wrench*. A boxed *set of ¼-inch drive sockets* can also be useful for working on some furniture and appliances.

A *small file* is useful for smoothing metal objects and for sharpening jobs. A *wood rasp* and a *sanding block* with a variety of sandpaper can be used for smoothing wood.

Buy a variety of *screwdrivers* and use them for driving and extracting screws. Do not use the screwdriver as a prybar for separating wood parts or for prying the lid off paint pails. You will damage the screwdriver and may damage the object you are working on, called a *workpiece*. Using the wrong size screwdriver can damage the screw head so it cannot be removed. Buy at least three sizes of both slot and Phillips tip screwdrivers, to handle any size screw.

For any wood-cutting chores buy a small *handsaw*. For all-around use choose a 10- or 12-point combination saw. For versatility in cutting you can buy a *saber saw* with a variety of blades that will cut wood, ceramic tile, or metal.

If you are putting together a very basic tool kit, consider the multi-use tools shown in camping or automotive catalogs. For example, tools are available in a plier configuration, but may have a wrench on the tip of one handle and a hammer on the tip of the other handle. One favorite tool is a Swiss army officer's knife, which has two knife blades, a screwdriver, a corkscrew, a scissors, a leather punch, a bottle opener, a can opener and even a toothpick in one small pocket knife. This knife is so handy it is used almost daily.

TOOL TIPS

Most product instruction sheets include a list of tools needed for assembly. Many how-to texts also include a list of tools needed to complete a particular project, to help you assemble the right tools before you start the job. This is intended to help you avoid that "7:00 p.m. Saturday" syndrome. That's the one where, at 7:00 p.m. on Saturday night, with one hour's work left to finish the job, you realize you don't have the tool(s) needed. The reason this always occurs at 7:00 p.m. on Saturday is because every hardware or tool store in the world closes at 6:00 p.m. Saturday.

CATALOGS

If you are a tool freak like me, it's fun to browse through tool catalogs to see the many special tools that are available. If you don't know what tools to buy for a particular job, describe your project to the tool store clerk, who can help you select the right tool for the job.

Some tool companies offer hard-to-find tools or tools at discount prices via their catalogs. A partial list of some companies that offer tools via catalogs follows. Some companies may charge a small fee for their catalog.

GARRETT WADE COMPANY, INC.
161 Avenue of the Americas
New York, NY 10013   (800) 221-2942

Fine tools, finishes, books.

TOOL CRIB
Div. of Acme Electric
1705 13th Avenue North
P.O. Box 1716
Grand Forks, ND 58206-1716   (800) 358-3096

A 170-page catalog of hand and power tools.

TOOLS ON SALE
Div. of Seven Corners Hardware, Inc.
216 W. 7th Street
St. Paul, MN 55102   (800) 328-0457

Everything: the catalog is 955 pages.

WOODHAVEN
5323 W. Kimberly Road
Davenport, IA 52806   (800) 344-6657

Uncommon woodworking tools.

THE WOODWORKER'S STORE
21801 Industrial Blvd.
Rogers, MN 55374   (612) 428-2199

A variety of shop tools and materials.

Buy quality wood chisels in widths of ¼ inch, ½ inch, and 3/4 inch, to do most home repairs. Workshop hobbyists will need a wider variety of chisel sizes.

Spring clamps shown, one of many clamps available, hold straightedge in place for marking, cutting off door.

TOOL LIST

If you are a homeowner and intend to do all or most of your own home maintenance chores, you'll need a fairly extensive tool chest. While we cannot anticipate every possible need, the following list is a reasonably complete roundup of the most common tools you'll buy, along with tips for using the tools.

CAULK GUN—An obvious must tool for applying caulks, but keep in mind that the most recent new product developments for making repairs in concrete, asphalt, and roofing also are caulk-tube products.

CHALK LINE — Consists of a teardrop-shaped chalk box, a mason's string, and a handle on the side of the box for rewinding the string (line). You can buy powdered chalk at the tool shop and refill the chalk box. Then, when you pull the line out of the chalk box, it is coated with chalk. You either have a helper hold the pull on the end of the line or (if working alone) drive a temporary nail in the workpiece to clip the end to. Then you position the extended chalk line between the two points where you want a mark or cutline. With the chalk line pulled tight between the two points, and lying lightly on the material you want to mark, you pick up the line at some point between the ends, and let go of the line. The taut line will snap back against the material and leave a straight line, marked by chalk dust, on the material. The problem is that the line often leaves a heavy layer of chalk dust, and the chalk is messy. It gets on your clothes and hands and materials where you don't want the chalk dust. If you leave excess chalk on wallboard, for example, it may be picked up in your latex or other paint and carried all over the wallboard surface by the paint roller. Or if you use the chalk line to mark the walls for installing a suspended ceiling, you will invariably get the chalk on your hands and spread it over the acoustic ceiling panels.

TIP: Pull the line out of the box and, holding the line in the air and away from any object you don't want marked, snap the line so the excess chalk flies off into midair. There will still be enough chalk left on the line to leave a mark but not enough to make a mess on everything.

CHISELS — Accidents happen when you try to force a dull tool to cut. Keep a fine grinding wheel handy and keep chisels sharp. Don't use the wood chisel for any purpose but cutting wood. Use a wood or plastic mallet to drive wood chisels. Don't drive a cold chisel (or any driven tool) with a carpenter's hammer: use a ball-peen or machinist's hammer.

CLAMPS — A variety of clamps is available for holding wood or other materials together while waiting until glue sets, or while drilling holes, for example. Common spring clamps that work like spring clothespins are useful for most clamping jobs. If you like to make picture frames, corner clamps are available that help you clamp two perpendicular work pieces together.

DRILL—Probably the most versatile tool you can have in the toolbox is the electric drill. In addition to drilling holes in almost any material, the drill can be fitted with dozens of accessories to do a wide array of repair tasks. By buying the right accessories you can drill, countersink, mix paint, sand, grind, polish, drive nuts, drive screws, and pump water or other fluids with this versatile tool. A good all-purpose drill choice for the homeowner is the $3/8$-inch reversible, variable-speed drill. For heavy-duty boring, rent or buy a $1/2$-inch drill. The modern variable-speed drills are a great improvement over the older, 1700 RPM models. High drill speeds are a drawback when using drills for anything but drilling. For example, for mixing paint, or with polishing or buffing wheels, or for drilling in hard materials such as steel, low RPM speeds are needed. High drill speeds also will dull drill bits instantly when

M47 model Black & Decker ³/₈-inch drill is an economical choice for most homeowner projects. Drill is reversible for removing bits and screws. Photo courtesy Black & Decker.

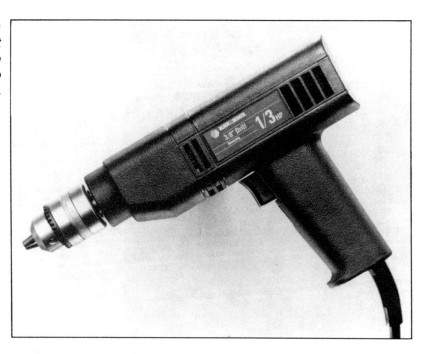

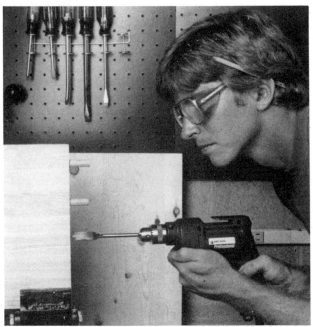

Pro model ³/₈-inch drill is variable-speed and reversible for all-round use. Wear eye goggles when working with tools. Photo courtesy Black & Decker.

The ELU™ Holgun Model 1186 drill is variable-speed reversible with power enough to drive plug cutters, hole saws, and screws. Photo courtesy Black & Decker.

Timberwolf drill has right-angle head for drilling at right angles in tight places, such as between studs or joists. Can be used where other drills will not fit. Photo courtesy Black & Decker.

Keyless chuck is one of many features that make this 3/8-inch drill model 7196 worth a look. Reversible and variable speed, no chuck key to lose or use, and Accu-Bore~ two-way level offer fast, accurate drilling. Photo courtesy Black & Decker.

Cordless Hammerdrill Model 1966R has two variable speed ranges to let you adjust the torque and speed for drilling concrete. Photo courtesy Black & Decker.

you are drilling in hard materials such as steel or masonry.

TIP: When drilling steel or concrete, use the variable-speed feature on your drill to keep the bit barely turning. Your impulse, when drilling in difficult material, is to open the drill speed to maximum. If the bit is not cutting, just spinning on the surface, it will overheat from the friction and dull quickly. This is why you see variable-speed pulleys on a drill press: drilling materials of different hardness requires different drill speeds. Use carbide masonry bits when drilling in masonry. It also helps to lubricate the tips of the drill bits: use a drop of oil on the bit tip when drilling metal; use water to cool and lubricate the bit when drilling in masonry.

FILES—A file is a tool that is used to remove or smooth metal. Files can be used to sharpen tools such as axes, shovels, or chisels. You can also use a file to "dress" or shape the edge of a damaged tool, such as reshaping the tip of a screwdriver.

GLUE GUN—Sometimes called a "hot melt" glue gun, these guns use sticks of glue that are melted by electrical power. The glues are fast-setting and can be used for a wide variety of repair jobs.

TIP: Hot glue is often useful when used in place of a clamp. Just put a drop of the glue on a workpiece and temporarily glue two objects together for shaping, sanding, drilling, or nailing.

GRINDER—A benchtop grinder is a useful tool for sharpening cutting tools such as chisels and hatchets, or for grinding and smoothing metal or other materials. Fit the grinder with wheels of vary-ing abrasive quality: a rough wheel can remove stock quickly; a smooth or fine abrasive wheel can be used for sharpening.

HAMMER, BALL-PEEN—A ball-peen hammer head has a hardened hammer face on one side and a ball on the other. Before modern fasteners such as Pop rivets were available, the ball side of the hammer was used to flatten or "peen" soft metal rivets (usually copper rivets). The hammer is a useful addition to the homeowner's tool box and can be used to drive steel chisels, masonry chisels, nail pullers, or concrete nails.

HAMMER, CARPENTER'S—Carpenter's hammers are made for driving and pulling nails. Do not use a carpenter's hammer as an all-purpose hammer. You can ruin a hammer by using it as a crowbar, or by driving chisels, star drills, or other hardened driving tools. Likewise, a carpenter's hammer is not heavy enough to drive hardened masonry nails; you may chip the head of your hammer, and the flying steel chip can injure an eye. Use a ball-peen or small sledge hammer for driving hardened concrete nails and with driven tools. Keep the face of the hammer head clean: grease, wax, or the coating from nails can coat the hammer face, causing the head to slip and bend nails. Always wear eye goggles when using any hammer, to avoid injury from flying nails or other objects.

TIP: Use a scrap of sandpaper to clean the hammer face frequently when you are working with adhesives, glues, coated nails, or any material that might coat the hammer face and cause it to slip when striking a nail.

HAMMER, SLEDGE—Large hammer used for heavy driving or for breaking concrete. The sledge hammer usually has two hammer faces, but may have a splitting wedge on one side of the head and a flat face on the other. A sledge hammer usually

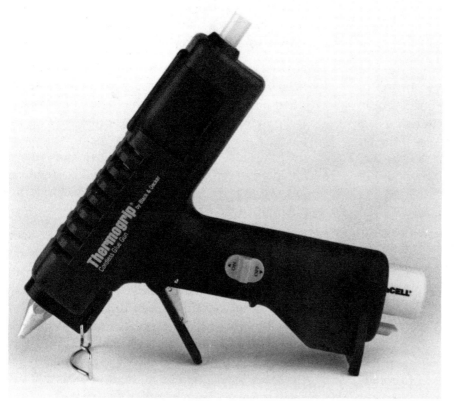

Thermogrip™ Cordless Glue Gun offers high portability for home repair or hobby projects. Photo courtesy Black & Decker.

Use a hand file or grinder to sharpen tools or to smooth rough metal edges.

Heavy-duty benchtop grinder can be fitted with wire or abrasive wheels for grinding or sharpening jobs. Wear goggles to protect eyes when grinding. Photo courtesy Black & Decker.

Grinding wheel can be chucked into a drill for portable grinding, here shown sharpening a lawn mower blade. Photo courtesy Black & Decker.

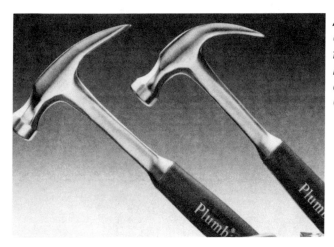

All-steel hammers by Plumb are available with either claw or rip (straight) style, have non-slip cushion grip for comfort. Buy a 16-ounce hammer for most household jobs, larger hammers (up to 28 ounces) for doing heavy framing or driving spikes. Photo courtesy Cooper Tools.

A claw hammer is the right tool for driving tools such as the nail set shown. If you are small, try buying a smaller hammer, such as a 14-ounce finishing hammer, to give your wrist a rest. Note eye goggles used when working with tools. Photo courtesy Black & Decker.

Model 9778 Heat Gun can also be fitted with a heat concentrator and scraper for use as a high-speed paint stripper. Photo courtesy Black & Decker.

Carpenter's 24-inch level has level vials on each end, plumb bubble in the middle, to help you build straight and plumb. Photo courtesy Stanley Tools.

has a head weight of 2 to 12 pounds or more.

HAMMER, WALLBOARD — I always advise anyone who is installing wallboard to use a wallboard screw gun and screws, not a hammer, for driving wallboard fasteners. The next-best advice would be: if you insist on nailing wallboard on, don't do so with a carpenter's hammer. The wallboard hammer is designed especially for that purpose, and its advantages make it well worth the price. First, the wallboard hammer has a larger face than a carpenter's hammer, and the hammer's face is crowned or convex. This larger, crowned face lets you set the wallboard nail below the surface of the board, or dimple it, without crushing the plaster core around the nail, and without cutting the face paper around the perimeter of the hammer mark. These two factors—crushing the plaster core and cutting or fracturing the face paper—account for a large percentage of the fastener failure problems in wallboard. The wallboard hammer handle is longer than an ordinary carpenter's hammer handle, so a person of average height can reach the top corner of the 8 foot high wall while standing on the floor. Because you are working continually in contact with large panels, you also will be forever bumping your knuckles if you use a carpenter's hammer.

TIP: Wallboard hammers have offset handles to protect knuckles. File or grind a crosshatch pattern on the face of the wallboard hammer. These slight face grooves help grip the nail head, and help you avoid slipping off the nail heads and bending the nails.

HEAT GUN—The electric heat gun is a useful tool for removing paint, thawing pipes, or loosening rusty nuts from bolts.

LADDERS — Never stand on a chair or other makeshift scaffold when doing home projects or repairs. An accidental fall is doubly dangerous when you are working with heavy or sharp tools that might add to the injury. Select a ladder of a proper height and observe all safety rules when climbing. Before buying, check the ladder's label for weight limitations of the ladder, and don't forget to consider not only your own weight but the weight of tools and materials you may carry up the ladder. Buy a Type 1 ladder, rated to support 250 pounds, or a Type 1A heavy-duty ladder that is rated to support 300 pounds, if you buy your clothes in Large sizes. Wear a tool belt with loops and pouches for carrying tools safely and keeping hands free for climbing. Keep your weight centered between the ladder rails: overreaching is a common cause of falls. Keep metal ladders away from electrical power lines.

TIP: Use cordless power tools when working on ladders or scaffold. Tool and extension cords are a tripping hazard when you are climbing.

LEVEL—A carpenter's level can be used to be sure a surface is level from side to side. It can also be used to check perpendicular surfaces for plumb (plumb is level or straight for perpendicular surfaces such as walls, door jambs, and fence or support posts). A 2-foot long carpenter's level is a good all-round choice for homeowners.

TIP: Smaller levels are useful for hanging pictures; for larger projects, you can tape a 2-foot long level to a longer, straight board to extend its reach and accuracy.

MALLETS—Mallets are hammers made with soft striking faces, and they are usually made of hardwood or plastic. These "soft hammers" are used to avoid damage when driving two sides of a wood joint together in furniture construction, for example. Mallets are also used to drive wood chisels to avoid damaging or "mushrooming" the head of the chisel. If you lack a mallet you can hold a block of wood over a wood surface you don't want to dent or mar, and hit the block of wood rather than the workpiece.

MEASURING TAPE—Cheap measuring tapes, or rules, are made for very infrequent use, and will not stand up to the wear and tear of a major remodeling job. Buy a tape that is at least 12 feet long: 16 or 25 feet is better. Check the blade of the tape to be sure the measurements are clearly visible; you will often be working in poor light when remodeling. Buy a tape with a wide blade that will stand stiff when the blade is extended: $3/4$-inch wide blades can be extended for measuring above your head, or down a wall, when you are working alone and don't have a helper to hold one end of the tape. Cheap tapes have small or weak lips or hooks at the end. They either slip off the edge of the workpiece each time you try to extend the tape or they break off easily.

TIP: Check the tip of the tape blade to be sure it is large and well-secured before making your purchase.

PAINT BRUSHES—Natural bristles such as hog bristles will become soft when exposed to water, so you must use natural bristle brushes only with oil base paints. For most applications, and always for use with latex paint, choose a paint brush with all-nylon bristles, or one having a blend of nylon and polyester bristles. Look the brush over carefully and spread the bristles apart to inspect between them. The brush handle should be smooth and shaped to fit the hand. The bristles should be attached to the handle with a non-corrosive metal ferrule—rust or other corrosion will ruin your paint job. Bristles should be separated with wood spacer plugs (not cardboard) from the metal ferrule. The bristle tips should be flagged, or split, and the bris-

tle ends should be chiseled or shaped for fine cutting. The brush size needed depends on the size of the job and the strength of the worker. If you do a lot of painting, both indoors and outdoors, you will need a variety of brushes. A 2-inch brush is useful for painting trim or other narrow surfaces. A 3-inch or 4-inch brush is best for painting large surfaces such as decks or siding. A tapered sash brush is best for painting small trim and window sash.

TIP: Use a spinner tool to clean both brushes and rollers. The spinner uses centrifugal force to fling all paint particles out of bristles or roller nap.

PAINT ROLLERS—Select a 9-inch roller frame that has nylon bearings and wire cage construction. Spin the roller cage with your hand to be sure it revolves easily. The roller handle end should be threaded to accept an extension handle. Choose roller covers made with synthetic fibers for most paint jobs. Choose a ¼-inch nap cover for painting flat, smooth surfaces where no texture is desired. Choose a $3/8$-inch nap cover for most wall and ceiling painting, and a 1-inch nap roller for painting stucco, texture, or other rough surfaces.

TIP: Use a mohair roller cover for applying varnish, polyurethane, or high-gloss alkyd paint finishes. The mohair roller will not leave any texture in the fine finishes.

PENCILS—What could you possibly learn about using so common a tool as a pencil? Especially in trim carpentry where cuts and miters must be exact, the pencil you use and the way you use it are critical. Pick up a carpenter's pencil for marking framing lumber and sheathing plywood. The heavier pencil and lead will last much longer than an ordinary lead pencil when used to mark rough surfaces. But for marking trim for cutting, the thickness of the pencil

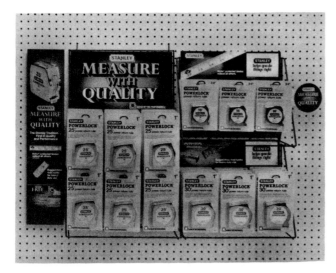

Select a measuring tape from this display rack. Choose a tape that is at least 12 feet long with a 3/4-inch wide blade for home remodeling chores. Photo courtesy Stanley Tools.

Quality 4-inch paintbrush has synthetic bristles with flagged tips to retain more paint and to provide smoother paint application. Brush ferrule is chromed to resist corrosion. Author photo.

Check roller frame to be sure the cage turns smoothly without binding. Handle should have threaded end for an extension handle. Select a roller cover to match the job: long-nap roller shown is right choice for painting stucco or rough-sawn wood. Author photo.

mark is crucial. You will often hear carpenters who work in pairs, with one person measuring and the other person cutting, say to "leave the mark" or "take the mark" when the cut is made. The saw blade itself can be $1/8$ inch thick, so even the width of a saw blade, when taken or left on either side of the pencil mark, can ruin a miter fit on trim. So use a #2 lead pencil for marking dimensions on trim lumber, and keep the pencil sharp so you know exactly where the cut should be.

TIP: For a super-sharp mark, screw a pencil sharpener to the underside of your workbench (so it's out of the way, not on the bench top) and sharpen the pencil frequently. Master trim carpenters go a step further: they also screw a pencil sharpener to the underside of the sawhorse that supports the miter saw, so they can put a fine point on the pencil after each cut.

PLANE—A tool used to smooth the surfaces on boards or to remove excess wood stock. Power planes are available for the serious workshopper; a small handheld block plane, costing about $20, will serve for most homeowner needs.

TIP: Many how-to texts advise to plane the edge on a sticking door. Keep in mind that the door originally was planed to fit into its frame, so any sticking is probably caused by loose hinges, sagging frames (usually seen only on older houses), and/or high humidity that has swelled the door so it sticks. If the door hinges are loose or the door is sagging, don't plane the door. Tighten the hinge screws to fix the problem. If high humidity is causing the door to swell and stick, the door will return to normal when dry weather returns. Thus, if you plane off too much wood, the door will fit loosely and be drafty when normal humidity conditions return, or when you have fixed the loose

hinge. You should thus sand or plane the door sparingly to avoid ruining the door.

POP™ RIVET TOOL—This tool is a must for joining metal parts together. The smallest model uses $1/8$-inch diameter collapsible rivets, available in a variety of lengths. The Pop™ rivet tool ("Pop" is a trademark) is very useful for repairing metal toys, and lawn, yard, or recreational equipment.

TIP: To remove rivets, choose a drill bit the same diameter as the rivet shank, usually $1/8$ inch. Drill through the center of the rivet head to pop the head off and punch out the rivet shank.

RAZOR KNIFE—One tool that is included on most tool lists, whatever job you're doing, is the razor knife. Use it to cut wallboard, floor covering, wall covering, vapor barriers, insulation, and building paper, and to sharpen your pencil. The problem is that cutting abrasive material, such as asphalt shingles or the core in wallboard panels, tends to dull the blade very quickly, and many people just will not throw those old blades away. You will work faster, be less tired, do a better job, and avoid tearing expensive materials such as wall covering if you change the blade whenever it gets dull, or at least at each coffee break. If you're doing a large project, you can buy replacement razor blades in packages of 100 blades. Or, if throwing the blades away seems poor economy, carry a pocket whetstone in your tool bag and sharpen the blade a few times before you discard it.

TIP: Wall covering wet with glue resists cutting and is easy to tear. To be sure you avoid damaging the covering, buy the knife with breakaway razor blades, and break off the blade after every cut to be sure you always have a sharp blade tip.

Pop Rivet Tool handles 1/8-inch diameter rivets, can be used for repairing rain gutters, toys, or cars. Photo courtesy Black & Decker.

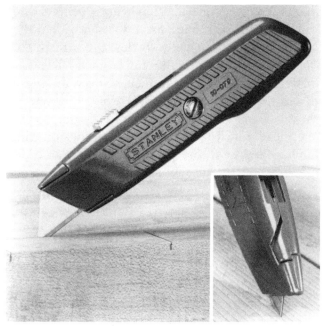

Stanley razor knife has a retractable blade for safe handling, stores extra blades in the non-slip handle. For safe cutting, sharpen or replace blade frequently. Photo courtesy Stanley Tools.

Skil Plunge Router has 1 3/4 HP motor, 2-inch cutting depth, and all ball bearings to stand up to your next project. Photo courtesy Skil.

Don't like manual sanding? Check out the QuickFinish™ model 7441 block sander by Black & Decker. Photo courtesy Black & Decker.

This ¼ sheet Palm Grip Sander (model 4011) has better balance for reduced vibration plus a through-the-pad dust collection bag. Has an optional adapter for a dust extraction hose. The sanding pad overhangs the motor housing to ensure flush sanding. Photo courtesy Black & Decker.

Shown is the ³/₈ sheet model 7453 sander with the dust extraction hose attached. You can hook the dust hose to most canister or shop vacuums for almost dust-free sanding. Photo courtesy Black & Decker.

A dust extraction hose attachment is a real plus when sanding soft materials such as wallboard compound. Photo courtesy Black & Decker.

Variable-speed belt sander has a dust collector and electronic speed control for heavy-to-fine sanding jobs. This model 7498 can tackle a variety of sanding applications. Photo courtesy Black & Decker.

For the toughest jobs you have, choose this 4½-inch sander/grinder model 9611 from Skil. Can be fitted with abrasive grinding wheels or sanding discs for sanding rι from car bodies or refinishing the wood deck. Photo courtesy Skil.

ROUTER—The router is a high-speed machine used for shaping molding or edging on furniture. It can also be used for cutting plastic laminates, using a laminate blade. A variety of bits permits you to choose any shape for the cut.

TIP: The laminate adhesive can stick in the laminate trimmer bit, pulling the blade into the edge of the laminate and damaging it. Spray your laminate trimmer bit with WD-40® so laminate adhesive will not stick to the bit.

SANDER — Your sanding needs may vary from using a small sanding block up to large power sanders used for shop projects. Small power sanders that will do most homeowner chores include half-sheet, orbital, and palm sanders that can be purchased for $30 or so.

SANDER/GRINDER—This tool is highly portable and can be equipped with any grade of sanding disk or grinding disk to grind rough concrete, stucco, plaster, rusty metal, or auto bodywork.

SAW, CIRCULAR — Buy a circular saw that can take a 6½- to 7¼-inch blade. This size is large enough to cut through nominal 2-inch stock (2 x 4s, etc.) when the saw is set at a 45° miter. Check the saw for weight and ease of handling before you buy it. Keep a sharp blade in the saw. Circular saw blades are made with teeth designed for ripping (cutting with the wood grain) or for crosscutting (cutting across the wood grain), or you can buy a combination blade that is a compromise for all-around use. A combination blade will do for most homeowners because they are not doing that much ripping, and they don't like to change blades that often. For paneling, however, buy and use the multi-tooth paneling blades. The fine-tooth blades eliminate splintering of the face ply on paneling. Never force a circular saw (or any power tool). The side pressure when you force a saw puts pressure on the motor shaft and bearings. You can buy circular saw blades for cutting almost any material, from steel to stone.

TIP: Invest $30 in a top-of-the-line, carbide-tipped saw blade. These offer long blade life and can be used for 90 percent of home projects.

SAW, HACK—Use the hack saw for cutting any kind of metal.

SAW, HAND—A hand saw or carpenter's saw will do most wood-cutting jobs. A good all-purpose saw might be the 12-tooth, 15-inch or 20-inch Shortcut saws by Stanley Tools (see photo).

SAW, HOLE—The hole saw can be chucked into a drill for cutting holes of various diameters in wood. The hole saw has a center mandrel or bit that serves as a pilot guide. Universal Quick-Change Mandrel from Black & Decker eliminates the need for a tightening nut. A common homeowner use for the hole saw is for installing a door lock.

SAW, SABER (JIG)—This tool, using a variety of specialty blades, can replace a host of other sawing tools. Fitted with a metal-cutting or hacksaw blade it will cut any metal; with grit blades you can cut ceramic tile, glass, and most metals; with wood-cutting blades it can be used as a keyhole saw; and those with scrolling features can replace a coping saw.

SCREWDRIVERS — Buy a variety of screwdrivers to cover all types and sizes of screws. At least three slot screwdrivers and three Phillips screwdrivers are necessary for ordinary household maintenance and repair. Don't try to drive Phillips-head screws with a slot screwdriver. The screwdriver may slip and injure you, or damage the screw or the workpiece. The big advance in screwdrivers is the development of wallboard screw guns and wallboard (drywall) screws. The screws are available in many sizes and can be used for building and

Pro model circular saw is the SawCat by Black & Decker. Fast depth adjustment and more powerful motor make it easy to use, capable of heavy-duty operation. Photo courtesy Black & Decker.

Use a hacksaw for cutting metal such as the electrical greenfield cable shown. Lacking a hacksaw, clamp a metal-cutting blade into your saber saw. Wear eye goggles. Photo courtesy Stanley Tools.

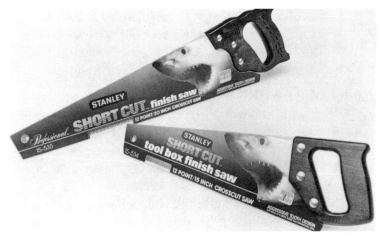

Stanley promises faster cutting action with either of their Short Cut™ finish saws. Choose either the 15-inch or 20-inch length for all-round household chores. Photo courtesy Stanley Tools.

Proper saw use is to "shake hands" with the handle, steady the workpiece with your free hand. It helps to have a helper to support the cutoff end. Photo courtesy Stanley Tools.

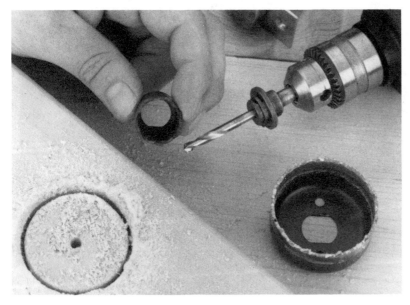

Universal Quick-Change Mandrel from Black & Decker lets you change hole saws without using a locking nut. Fits all carbon steel hole saws, so you don't have to buy two hole saw mandrels. Photo courtesy Black & Decker.

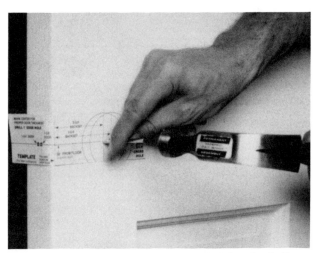

Shown in these four photos is Black & Decker's Door Lock Installation Kit. Use the latch locator pin to start drill holes on the lock template. Photo courtesy Black & Decker.

Use the hole saw to bore the lock hole, using the pilot hole as a guide. Photo courtesy Black & Decker.

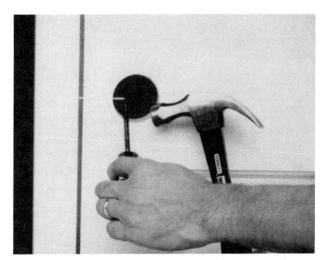

Patented drill guide ensures properly aligned pilot holes for accurate hole saw drilling. Photo courtesy Black & Decker.

Drill out both the lock and latch holes in the door. Then use the latch locator pin, pushed through the latch hole, to mark the spot on the jamb for the latch hole. Photo courtesy Black & Decker.

Scrolling jig saw model 7572 has a 3.5 amp motor, two speeds, and auto-scrolling action for cutting intricate designs. Photo courtesy Black & Decker.

Electronic variable-speed jig saws such as Black & Decker's models 7568 and 7588 maintain selected cutting speed in a variety of materials. Built-in blade storage holds up to twelve blades for easy retrieval. Photo courtesy Black & Decker.

Skil calls their adjustable jig saw the Vari-Orbit. Has six orbit positions, 45° tilting foot, variable speed, and it's double insulated. Photo courtesy Skil.

Compound miter saw has telescoping rails for easy operation. Aluminum fence has four cast holes for mounting jigs and clamps. Photo courtesy Black & Decker.

Specialty saw blades, such as the Piranha™ blade for sawing treated deck lumber, let you use power circular or miter saws for a wide range of jobs. Photo courtesy Black & Decker.

hanging cabinets, or installing door hinges, or for building almost any project from shelves to storage sheds. Be careful when working in damp places, where you might get a dangerous shock; be careful also when you are using power tools on ladders or scaffold, where tool power cords can tangle underfoot and cause a fall.

TIP: Choose a cordless, battery-powered screw gun or drill to eliminate any danger from shock in damp work places and to eliminate dragging electrical cords up ladders. Cordless tools are a good investment in safety.

SQUARE, CARPENTER (RAFTER) — A carpenter or rafter square can be used to check lumber and other materials to see if they are square. Quality squares will have rules with $1/16$-inch and $1/8$-inch gradations on the face, $1/12$-inch and $1/16$-inch gradations on the back. The tongue or small leg of the square is 16 inches long and 1 inch wide, while the body or long leg of the square is 24 inches long and 2 inches wide. This makes the square a handy layout tool for framing either in 24 inches on center (o.c.) or 16 inches on center spacings. If you are really serious about learning to use the square it is about as handy as a calculator, after you know how to use the rafter tables, brace measure, octagon scale, and board measure.

SQUARE, COMBINATION—A combination or machinist's square combines a 1-foot steel ruler plus an adjustable base that lets you mark either square (90°) or 45° miters. The base contains a level plus a metal scribe pin that can be used for marking wood or metal.

T-SQUARE — Sometimes referred to as a wallboard T-square, this is one of the most useful tools

Cordless screwdriver provides enough torque for chores such as hanging drapery rods or removing cabinet hardware before painting. Photo courtesy Black & Decker.

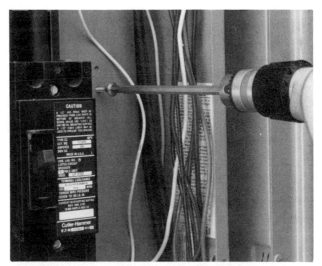

Extension bits let you work around obstacles or in recessed areas. The 3½-inch to 6-inch long Scorpion bits are available with either slot or Phillips tips. Photo courtesy Black & Decker.

Do you work with a one-size-fits-all screwdriver? Reduce the frustration factor: buy a selection such as this 10-piece screwdriver set by Stanley. Photo courtesy Stanley Tools.

A small square such as the try square shown can be handy for shop projects. An option is to buy the combination or machinist's square that features a miter guide and a level in the base. Photo courtesy Stanley Tools.

you can own. If you do any cutting on wallboard, plywood, paneling, or any panel that is 4 feet wide, this tool is indispensable. The only warning is that you must avoid getting your free hand in the way when cutting along the T-square; if the razor knife slips you can get a nasty injury.

TIP: When cutting wallboard or any material with a razor knife, with the material leaning against a wall, hold the top of the T with your free hand, keeping the free hand well out of the line (to the side) of the knife cut. Place the toe of your work shoe against the bottom end of the T-square to keep it from slipping sideways. Cut from the top down, halfway across the width of the panel. Now reverse the knife and cut from the bottom edge of the panel up, so you are pulling the knife away from, not towards, your foot. When using the T-square as a

cutting guide for power tools, use clamps to hold the T-square in place. This way, if the T-square or the saw or other cutting tool slips, you won't have a hand in the way.

TOOL BAGS—If you do major remodeling work, invest in the pro-type leather tool bags. Some come already riveted to a web belt; some you will find loose in bins at cut rates. Buy a web canvas-type military belt, a bag for holding nails or screws, and a tool holder. Rivet the two leather bags on the belt so they won't slip; the two bags should be worn so they are off the hip, not worn in front of your belly. Nail and tool bags carried in your middle get in the way when you bend over. You can also injure yourself if you bend over with sharp tools carried in the range of your midsection. Don't overload the belt with extra nails, screws, or tools—you'll have to carry that weight.

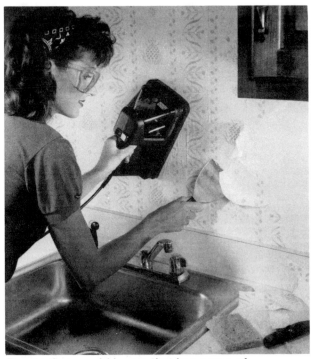

Renovating an old house that has acres of wallpaper? This tool, dubbed the Steamworks™ by Black & Decker, is claimed to work faster and neater than rental steam units, and you don't have to pay the rent. Photo courtesy Black & Decker.

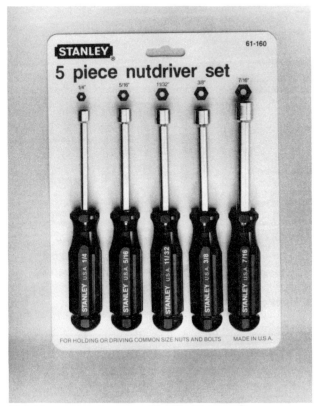

Nutdriver set helps you drive the five most common nuts used around the house. If you're raising children and are stuck with those "easy assembly" toys, this is definitely for you. Photo courtesy Stanley Tools.

Adjustable or Crescent® wrench can handle odd-sized nuts in hard-to-reach places. Shown tightening the hardware on an old garage door. Photo courtesy Black & Decker.

Seldom-used tools can be rented. The power washer can be used for a multitude of cleaning jobs from preparing an asphalt drive for sealing to cleaning house siding prior to painting. Photo courtesy Black & Decker.

Retaining wall looking shabby? Clean it with wood cleaner and power wash to remove mildew and dirt. Let it dry, then seal with a water repellent. Photo courtesy Black & Decker.

TIP: If you are slim-hipped and the tool bags won't stay put around your waist, attach a pair of canvas carpenter's suspenders to the belt to help support the weight and keep the belt around your waist.

WALLPAPER STEAMER — Small, handheld steamers can replace the bulky rental units for removing wallpaper quickly.

WRENCHES—Wrenches are needed to assemble/dismantle objects that are held together by nuts and bolts, or for separating threaded pipes. At the least, you should have a 6-inch adjustable wrench. Also useful is a small kit containing a ¼-inch socket drive and sets. If you will be doing any plumbing on threaded pipes you will need a pair of pipe wrenches (you have to use two: one wrench to hold the pipe or fitting from turning while you unscrew the other fitting or pipe). A pair of 10-inch pipe wrenches will let you do most plumbing maintenance jobs.

TOOL RENTAL

One alternative to buying expensive tools for occasional use is to rent the tools. Rental equipment stores in major cities offer everything from backhoe tractors for digging your own basement to rotary sewer cleaners like the pros use. Your problem is to decide whether you have the expertise to use the tool after paying the rental, or if hiring a pro makes sense. Not everyone can clean a sewer and walk away with a clean uniform just because they have the right equipment.

The best way to decide whether to rent the tool or hire a pro is to get a bid from the pro, and check the rental cost of the tool(s) at the store. Renting tools can be expensive, because the job invariably will take more time than you estimate. Those half-day rental rates quoted by tool rental companies can be misleading, because you seldom can do a job and get the tool returned within a four to six hour period.

The first rule, if you decide to rent a tool, is to be very sure that the job has reached the stage where using the rental tool is the next step. You do not want to pay rental rates while the tool lies unused. The second rule is to finish the job and return the tool immediately. If you leave the tool lying around instead of returning it, you pay a heavy penalty for the delay.

Tools You Can Rent

Tools you might consider renting include:

- ❏ 10-pound sledge for breaking concrete
- ❏ Reciprocating saw (useful for disassembly when remodeling, or for cutting in difficult locations)
- ❏ Portable grinder
- ❏ Floor or other heavy-duty sanders
- ❏ Paint sprayers
- ❏ Angle drill (has a 90° angle on the chuck, to let you drill pipe or wire holes between studs or joists, for example)
- ❏ Power hammer (uses powder charges to drive fasteners in steel or concrete)
- ❏ Miter saw (power or hand, for fine trim or molding cuts)
- ❏ Texture machine (for spraying textures, stucco)

Check with your local tool rental outlet for a complete list of rental tools available. In addition to conventional tool rental firms, many specialty stores will rent or loan you the tools you need. For example, ceramic tile dealers usually will loan you the tools to install the tile you buy there; paint and wall covering dealers loan wall covering tools.

2.
Organizing a Home Shop

For the dedicated woodworker, the need for workshop space can sometimes get out of hand. If the shop is to hold a variety of stationary power tools, such as a radial arm saw, a drill press, and a lathe, you must multiply the amount of needed floor space, allow room on all sides for maneuvering plywood and lumber, include space for storing materials and tools, make extra electrical power provisions for all the power tools, and take steps to increase soundproofing between the shop and living spaces. But when organizing space for general home maintenance the home shop need not be elaborate. You should, however, set aside a designated area for storing tools and materials, and keep the home repair clutter limited to one space.

LOCATION

When selecting the location for your shop or work area, keep in mind such factors as sawdust, dirt, odor, and noise problems. Furnace blowers can pick up fumes, odors, dust, and other debris through the ducts, and circulate them through the house. Furnace ducts can also provide conduits for noise transfer. If you have a forced-air furnace, consider having supplementary shop heaters to avoid having ducts and air registers in the work area. Build curtain walls with doors, and use fiberglass batt insulation in walls or ceilings between the shop and living areas to help control noise and dirt. Caulking any cracks where noise might leak past will help soundproof the shop area. Also, if you have stationary tools, place rubber pads under base legs to reduce noise from tool vibration.

POWER REQUIREMENTS

Basic requirements for a work area include adequate electrical power outlets to accommodate all electric power tools. Multiple outlets are needed, on separate circuits, so you don't trip the circuit breakers and don't have to disconnect one tool to use another. Obviously, all electrical outlets should be grounded.

Ground fault circuit interrupters (GFCIs) can protect you against dangerous electrical shocks while you are standing well-grounded on concrete floors in the basement or garage workspace. Keep in mind that a grounded circuit alone will not protect the operator from dangerous or fatal electrical shock. This the reason is why we have ground fault circuit interrupters. The GFCI senses even a small ground or loss of electricity, long before the current level is high enough to harm a person, and shuts down the current flow in the circuit before injury can happen to the operator. GFCIs are mandatory by electrical code in any area where there is a high risk of electrical shock, such as bathrooms, laundry areas, kitchens, and other areas where water is present.

LIGHTING

In addition to having adequate electrical outlets, the space should be wired to provide for a well-lit work area. For your safety it is important to be able to light the workpiece and to avoid injury from a power tool or from a slipped chisel or other hand tool. At a minimum, you should install 4-foot long, overhead fluorescent shop lights above the workbench or tool area. These twin-tube fluorescent shop lights are available at home centers at a cost of $10 each or less. A flexible gooseneck-type desk lamp can be used to focus light on small workbench projects. Spot lighting with a portable work light, such as the mechanic's light with a retractable power cord, should also be provided to ensure proper lighting and good visibility in the workplace.

SAFETY

Another welcome addition, especially if your shop has a concrete floor, is a rubber floor pad or mat. The rubber pad will cushion your feet and make long-term standing more comfortable and less tiring for feet and legs. A rubber floor pad underfoot may also provide additional insurance against elec-

trical shock when you are operating power tools.

If possible, build walls around your shop area so there are doors that can be closed and locked when the shop is left unattended. Especially if young children are about, sharp tools and toxic materials present a real home hazard. Another safeguard is to equip your shop with a master switch, so you can with a flick of one switch easily shut down electrical power to the entire area when you are not at work. This way, electrical tools cannot be activated by inquisitive shop intruders.

Because of use of wood and chemicals in the shop area, there is always a possibility of fire. Install a smoke alarm in your shop, on a wall near the ceiling. Also, hang a fire extinguisher on the shop wall as a fire safety precaution. Buy toxic materials only in small quantities, and observe all manufacturers' label directions for handling, storage, and disposal of chemicals.

One serious mistake made by people doing home repairs is to use a chair as a ladder for reaching high places. This is an extremely dangerous practice and should be avoided. Chairs are constructed to support the average person's weight while sitting. A standing person may exert undue weight on the legs of the chair or on the seat, and tip the chair or break through the seat material. Buy or build a step stool and stand on it while doing any repairs that you cannot reach while standing on the floor. The step stool is also useful for hanging draperies or curtains, or for hanging pictures or mirrors. For projects that are far above the floor, use a sturdy step or extension ladder (see "Ladders," in Chapter 1, Tools).

Another useful item that can serve as a safe platform for sawing is a sawhorse. Many people may think it safe to use any handy platform, such as the steps on a ladder, as a base to hold materials that are being sawn. But wood that is improperly supported for power sawing can kick back with great force and injure the saw operator, or it can slip and

A corner of a basement or garage can serve as shop space for storing tools and materials and for maintaining the home. Photo courtesy Clairson International.

permit the worker to lose control of the saw, with devastating consequences. You can build your own sturdy sawhorses, following the plans shown. If you will use them as a sawing platform, you'll need a pair of sawhorses.

As an alternative to building the sawhorses from scratch, check out the fiberglass or metal sawhorse brackets that are available at home center stores. Using the brackets, all you'll have to do is to cut the 2 x 4 legs and crosspieces to the desired length, then nail the pieces together through the brackets.

TOOL STORAGE

A 4' x 8' panel of pegboard, plus a supply of wire tool hangers, can hold most of your necessary hand tools, keeping them easily accessible while protecting them from damage. Fasten the pegboard at the top of the wall above the workbench so tools are readily accessible for adults but high enough to be out of reach of small children.

KEEP IT CLEAN

Buy a shop vacuum and keep it handy for cleaning up sawdust and other shop debris. Keep the workplace clean to avoid having dirt and dust tracked through the house. If you have no other finish on concrete floors, apply a clear concrete floor sealer to stop concrete dusting and to repel any spilled materials. Make floors easy to clean by sealing the concrete so spilled liquids won't penetrate and stain the concrete.

YOUR WORKBENCH

Finally, you'll need a workbench. Many workbench kits are available at your home center or lumber dealer. These kits often consist of a metal frame and legs that can be assembled using bolts supplied with the kits. Then you must cut a bench top from plywood or particle board, and secure it with screws provided.

An alternative is to build your own workbench, using all wood. Shown is a plan for a workbench that you can build using ordinary hand and power tools. The plan is for The Stanley Workbench, developed by the Stanley Tool folks. Stanley points out that this is a sturdy, professional-quality workbench that is rugged enough to stand up to all your do-it-yourself projects. Stanley recommends that you build the bench where you intend to use it, because the bench is large and may not fit through doors, halls, or stairways. You can see from the

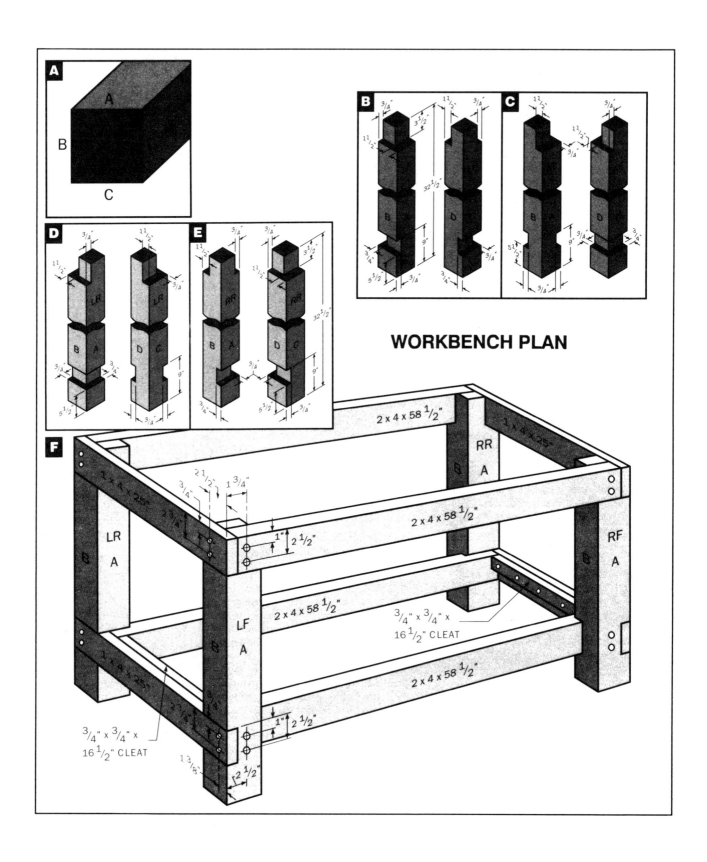

WORKBENCH PLAN

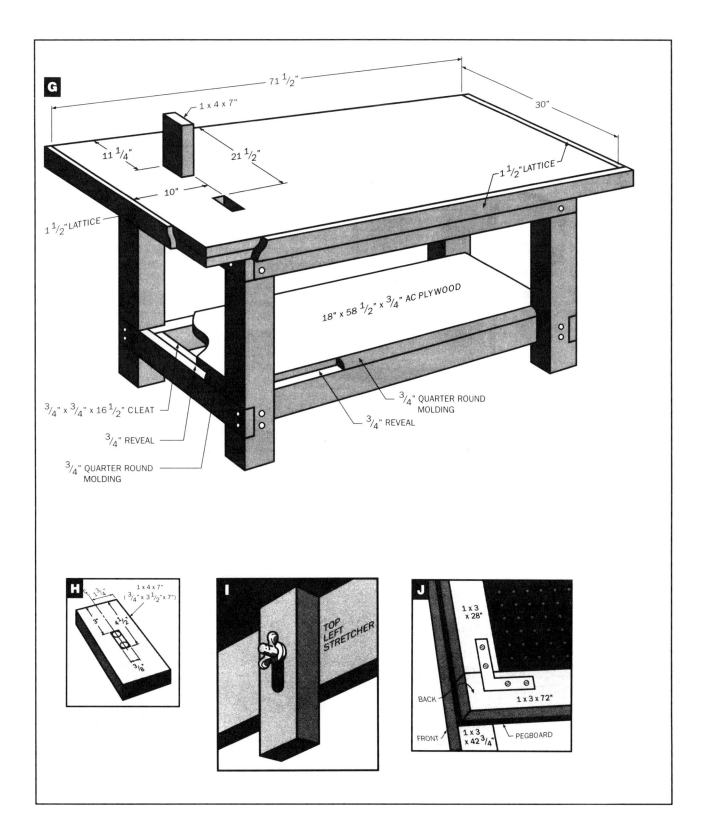

G

71 1/2"

30"

1 x 4 x 7"

11 1/4"

21 1/2"

1 1/2" LATTICE

10"

1 1/2" LATTICE

18" x 58 1/2" x 3/4" AC PLYWOOD

3/4" QUARTER ROUND MOLDING

3/4" REVEAL

3/4" x 3/4" x 16 1/2" CLEAT

3/4" REVEAL

3/4" QUARTER ROUND MOLDING

H
1 x 4 x 7"
(3/4" x 3 1/2" x 7")
3/4"
3"
4 1/2"
3/8"

I
TOP LEFT STRETCHER

J
1 x 3 x 28"
BACK
1 x 3 x 72"
FRONT
1 x 3 x 42 3/4"
PEGBOARD

WORKHORSE PLAN

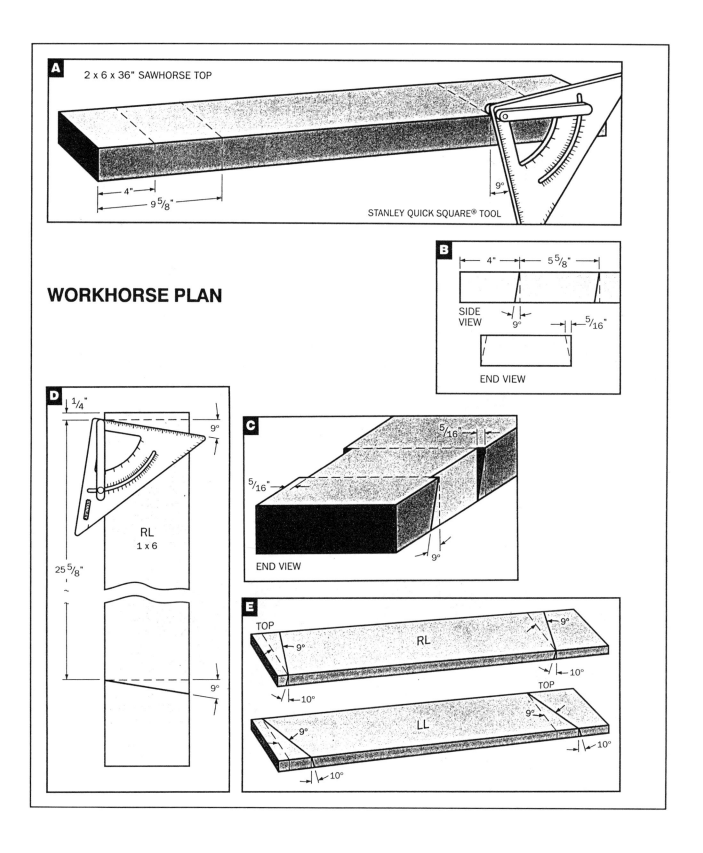

A 2 x 6 x 36" SAWHORSE TOP

4"

9 5/8"

9°

STANLEY QUICK SQUARE® TOOL

B 4" 5 5/8"

SIDE VIEW

9°

5/16"

END VIEW

D 1/4"

9°

RL
1 x 6

25 5/8"

9°

C 5/16"

5/16"

END VIEW

9°

E TOP

9°

RL

9°

10°

10°

TOP

9°

LL

9°

10°

10°

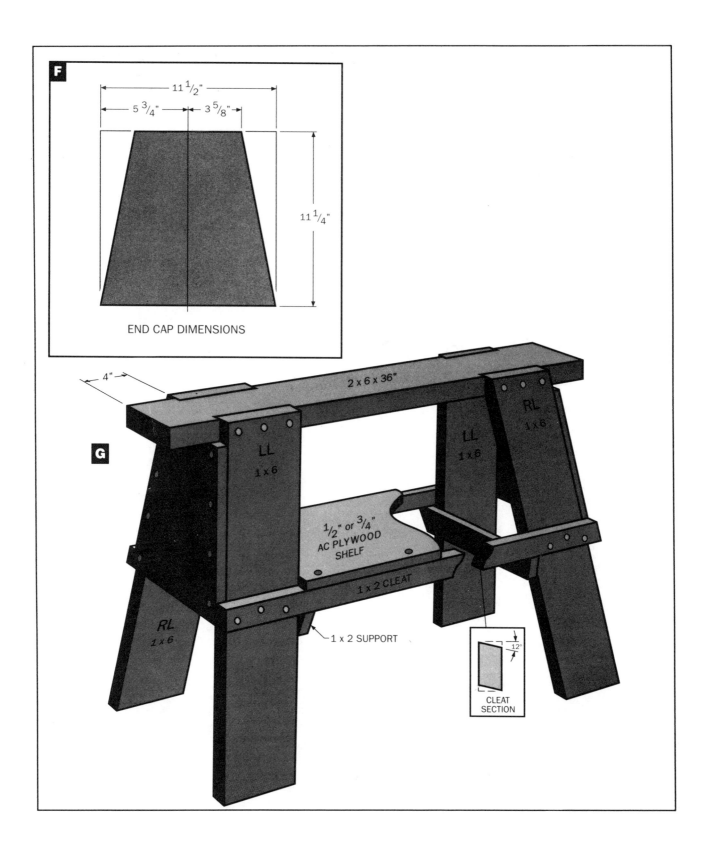

F

11 1/2"

5 3/4"   3 5/8"

11 1/4"

END CAP DIMENSIONS

G

4"

2 x 6 x 36"

RL
1 x 6

LL
1 x 6

LL
1 x 6

RL
1 x 6

1/2" or 3/4"
AC PLYWOOD
SHELF

1 x 2 CLEAT

1 x 2 SUPPORT

12°

CLEAT
SECTION

drawings how easily this project goes together, and at the time of this writing Stanley also offers a 28-minute video tape on how to build the bench. The offer is good while video supplies last, from: The Stanley Works, Advertising Services, Box 1800, Dept. WBB, New Britain, CT 06050.

One trick you might consider is to nail a layer of $\frac{1}{8}$-inch hardboard to the top of your workbench, over the plywood. When the top becomes stained or damaged you can simply remove the hardboard and discard it. Cut and install a new piece of hardboard atop the bench and you will have a clean, new work surface.

Also shown is the Stanley sawhorse. Build a pair of these sturdy sawhorses to serve as a firm foundation for all your home repair tasks.

3.
Fasteners and Connectors

Whether a family drinks coffee or not, it's a safe bet almost every house in the country has a 2-pound coffee can. This can is a catchall that holds every bent nail or leftover screw ever generated by home repair or assembly projects. When a nail, screw, or bolt is needed, the do-it-yourselfer dumps out the contents of the coffee can and searches through the mess for an all-purpose fastener that might solve whatever problem is at hand. Of course, the fastener is always the wrong size and/or type, and often ruins the project. Using the wrong nail will split the wood; forcing a screw that is a "close fit" will strip the screw hole at best and mar or damage the workpiece at worst.

So the first advice about fasteners is: buy one of those compartmentalized plastic or metal organizers, and fill the drawers with a selection of the most-used nails, screws, and bolts for your household. Many home centers will offer such an organizer, complete with an assortment of "most wanted" fasteners. Buying such an assortment is one of the best investments you can make toward making faster, better home repairs. Your repair projects will go much more smoothly, with far more professional results, if you have the proper fastener for the job.

NAILS

Consider this: I have a nail catalog the cover of which proclaims that it lists "over 10,000 types and sizes of nails." If one type or size of nail would do all jobs, manufacturers would only make one nail. The nails are made from different metals, in different sizes, lengths, styles, and finishes. In addition, the nails vary by the shape and style of the head and by the shape of the point. We'll explore these variations in nails and explain why certain features are important.

Metals

Most nails are made of mild steel, for nailing wood and other building materials together. For nailing very hard materials, such as nailing into concrete or hardwood flooring, hardened or case-hardened steel nails are preferable. Aluminum nails are used for fastening aluminum, and they also offer non-corrosive benefits for building decks or for installing exterior siding. Keep in mind that aluminum nails cost more per pound than steel nails, but this is at least partially offset by the fact that aluminum is lightweight, so there are more aluminum nails in a pound. Less often seen are brass and copper nails. These nails may be used for decorative purposes or for their non-corrosion qualities. Brass and copper nails and screws are often used in boat building because they resist rust.

Finishes

Nails intended for general use in building or interior finishing are left with a shiny or "bright" finish. For greater holding power the nails may be "cement coated" with an adhesive. If the nail is to be used for exterior projects, such as fences or decks or for attaching door or window casing, it must be rust resistant. These nails will be zinc-coated, either by being hot dipped or electroplated with zinc. Nails that will be purposely exposed to moisture during the building process, such as lath nails that will be covered with wet plaster or wallboard nails that will be covered with taping compound, may be "blued." Other weather-resistant nails may be made of stainless steel or may be cadmium plated.

Heads, Points

Nail heads are shaped so they will best perform their intended task. Nails that must hold soft materials, such as asphalt shingle nails, have large heads to resist tearing out. Carpet tacks have large heads for the same reason that roofing nails do. Nails for metal roofing have large heads but also have a neoprene washer to seal the nail hole against moisture penetration. Nails that will hold wood together do not need as large a head; thus, the smaller round head on common and box nails.

Finish and casing nails hold wood together, but we want to conceal the heads; thus the heads are smaller so they can be sunk below the surface of the finish wood. Nail heads that will be driven flush with the workpiece may be cupped or countersunk. The duplex or scaffold (double-headed) nail is made to

hold scaffold (staging) or concrete forms temporarily together. The nails can be pulled by prying on the second head when forms or scaffolding are dismantled.

Nail points also vary according to their intended use. The most common nail point is the diamond point. Also available are the chisel, blunt, needle, screw, and ring points. Chisel and blunt points are used to cut through the wood fibers rather than following the grain and splitting the wood. A common carpenter's trick is to blunt a nail with a diamond point by placing the point on concrete or steel and striking the nail head. It's easier, of course, to buy nails with blunt points. An alternative to using blunt points that avoid splitting wood is to pre-drill the nail holes before driving the nails. When trimming you can put a nail in the drill chuck and use it as a bit for pre-drilling the nail hole. Use a nail as a bit that is the same size as the nail you are driving; i.e., use a 4d finish nail to pre-drill for 4d nails, a 6d nail to pre-drill for using a 6d finish nail.

Types

The nail most often used for framing and general purposes is the Common nail. Another type, called the Box nail, has a thinner shank than the Common nail to avoid splitting wood. Casing nails have shanks like Box nails, have heads similar to but slightly larger than Finishing nails, and are used to nail casings around doors or windows. Finishing nails have a small brad head that can be driven beneath the surface of trim or cabinetry, and they have diamond points.

Roofing nails have large heads, and some have barbed shanks for better holding power. Some roofing nails have neoprene washers (use these for nailing fiberglass roof panels onto a porch or deck roof, for example). Because they are exposed to moisture, roofing nails are galvanized to help them resist rusting and corrosion. If you are nailing a new, second layer of shingles over an existing shingled roof (not removing the old layer of shingles) be sure you advise the dealer, so he can help you select the proper nail length to go through two layers of shingles.

Special nails available include the Duplex or double-head scaffold nail. These nails have a primary head that can be driven tight against the wood to hold it in position. The secondary head is provided to let you easily pull the nail when you want to dismantle the scaffold or remove wood forms from around a concrete project. Use these nails for any temporary project that will be dismantled at a later date.

Ring-shanked nails can be used for installing floor underlayment, shakes, or wallboard. The ring-shank has "threads" on the shank that provide superior holding power to resist "popping" or pull-out. This superior holding power is necessary to prevent nail heads from popping and ruining the appearance of the finished project. For example, popped nail heads in underlayment will show as ugly bulges under vinyl floor covering; popped nail heads on wallboard will show up as bulges of raised and cracked taping compound over the nail heads and will ruin your decorating job.

Hardened fluted or cut nails are used for nailing wood or other materials to concrete. For example, if you are nailing wood furring strips to a concrete block wall you should use flat concrete nails, driven into the mortar joints between the blocks. For nailing 2 x 4 wall sole plates to a poured concrete floor, fluted (round) shank concrete nails penetrate and hold best. For even easier fastening to concrete, buy or rent a power nail driver that uses cartridge-type gunpowder charges to drive the steel fasteners. These powder charges vary in size and explosive power, depending on the fastening job; i.e., power-driving a fastener into a concrete block mortar joint is much easier than driving a heavy retaining bolt for wrought iron into a hardened concrete porch surface. Ask the dealer or tool rental agent for help in choosing the right charge and fastener for your particular job.

Spiral or screw shank nails for hardwood flooring are hardened to drive easier without bending, and have greater holding power due to their shank styles. Special nailing guns are also available for use on hardwood flooring. These guns have a magazine for holding a special nail package not unlike the cartridge clip on a rifle. The nailing tool has a special lip at the bottom of the cylinder. The lip is positioned over the edge of the flooring to align the tool. A mallet is provided with the tool. When you position the tool over the edge of the flooring and strike the plunger with the mallet, a nail is driven into the tongue of the flooring. The blow of the mallet does two things: it drives the flooring board tight against the next board and drives the nail at the same time. You cannot use an air-driven nail gun for nailing hardwood flooring, because the air gun will not drive the two flooring boards up tightly together, and you will have gaps or cracks at the joints.

There are also cement-coated standard nails, called "coolers," that can be hand-driven but are designed for use in air-driven power nailers. Cement-coated countersunk nails, sometimes called "sinkers," have a resin cement coating that softens from the heat and friction generated when the nail is driven. The cement then hardens and helps hold the nail against popping.

Nail Size

Nail sizes are indicated by a penny (d) designation. The 2d or 2 penny nail is 1 inch long; from the 2d up to the 16d nail, each penny increase means a ¼-inch increase in length. For example, 2d = 1 inch; 3d = 1 ¼ inches; 4d = 1½ inches, etc. (See chart for nail sizes and number per pound.) Above the 20d designation, at lengths of 4 inches or more, nails are called spikes. After the 4 inch, 20d, comes the 30d, at 4½ inches; the 40d spike at 5 inches; and the 50d spike at 5½ inches long. Spikes are used to fasten timbers, or for any job where a nail with a long shank or reach is needed: rain gutters, for example, are hung with gutter spikes.

Choosing Nail Length

Unless you want to clinch the nail on the backside of the wood nailed, you must choose a nail that is shorter than the combined thickness of the two boards being nailed, so the nail will not penetrate completely through both boards. To find the maximum length (penny or "d") of nail to use, figure the thickness of the board to be nailed, expressed in eighths of an inch. For example, to nail a board that is ½ inch thick, figure $^4/_8$ = 4d = 1½ inch nail. This length means the nail will go through the ½-inch board being nailed and penetrate 1 inch into the second board.

Nailing Tips to Remember

❏ Always nail the thinner board to the thicker board.

❏ Clean the face of the hammer head with sandpaper to remove glue and dirt and to prevent bending nails.

❏ To avoid splitting the wood when driving finishing nails, use one of the nails as a drill bit for pre-drilling nail holes.

❏ Use carpenter's wax (beeswax, available at home centers) to lubricate the nail for easier driving. Beeswax also works for lubricating screws.

❏ Use a mash (small sledge) or a ball-peen hammer for driving hardened nails in concrete.

❏ Drive cut concrete nails into mortar joints,

NAIL CHART

"D" (penny)	Length	Number per pound Common	Finish
2	1"	875	1,300
3	1¼"	575	850
4	1½"	315	600
5	1³/₄"	265	500
6	2"	190	300
7	2¼"	160	—
8	2½"	105	200
9	2³/₄"	90	—
10	3"	70	120
12	3¼"	60	110
16	3½"	50	90

NOTE: Nails smaller than 1" are called "brads." Larger nails are called "spikes."

not into the concrete block in basement walls. The nails will simply break a hole if driven into the hollow block: they will hold firmly if driven into the solid mortar joint.

❏ Use round hardened concrete nails when driving into a solid concrete floor. Use a masonry bit to pre-drill the hole; use a 2-pound sledge to force the nail home.

❏ Use the right nail for the job. For example, the head on a shingle nail is the wrong shape for nailing wallboard, and it will cut through the wallboard and fail. Also, latex paint will often discolor and leave a yellow ring over the galvanized nail head, when shingle nails are used for wallboard.

❏ Toenailing, or joining two pieces of wood at right angles to each other by driving the nails at an angle, results in a very weak joint and possible failure because of splitting the wood. Toenailing is permissible only when the joint will not be subjected to stress. Use metal connectors for joining wood at right angles.

❑ To putty nail holes in trim, when using oil base wood putty, first apply wood sealer or stain and sealer to the wood. Then putty the nail holes. Finally, apply finish coats of varnish or polyurethane. If you putty nail holes before sealing the wood, the oil in the putty will leach into the wood and leave circular stains around each nail hole.

SCREWS AND BOLTS

Screws and bolts are used as fasteners, rather than nails, because they have better holding power and resist pullout better than nails. Screws and bolts are also preferred for many applications because they can be removed if you want to disassemble the project at a future date.

The development of the power screw gun for wallboard installation has sparked a corresponding increase in the development and use of screws of all kinds.

All-purpose screws are often referred to as "drywall" or "wallboard" screws, though actually many of these are too long for use with wallboard. Use screws for building almost any project: cabinets, furniture, fences, decks, gazebos, and storage sheds can all be assembled with rust-resistant screws.

Screws for power driving have Phillips heads, or slots with the familiar "X" shape. This type of head is more easily gripped with the screwdriver tip than the straight slot-head screw with its single cross groove tip. The "X" groove in the Phillips head makes the screwdriver tip self-centering, which results in less chance that the screwdriver tip can slip out of its slot and damage the screw head or the workpiece.

A more recent screw development is the torx-head, which has an hourglass-shaped groove in the head to receive this special bit. The torx screw is most often seen in automotive applications. For example,

the headlight retaining screws on cars often have torx heads.

Screw Heads and Gauges

Screws are available with flat, round, oval, or countersunk heads, with either Phillips or slot grooves for driving. Screws are also designated by "gauge" or shank size, and by length. See the screw chart for a review of screw lengths, gauges, and diameters.

Lag screws are fasteners that have screw threads for driving, but rather than having a slot for a screwdriver they have a square or hexagonal head that can be driven with a wrench or socket and power driver. Lag screws are commonly used for securing joists to beams, or for securing a ledger joist for a deck to the framing on the side of a house. Other uses for lag screws include securing posts and rails to a deck and for securing joists to deck posts.

SCREW CHART	
Length	**Gauge Numbers**
¼"	0-3
³/₈"	2-7
½"	2-8
⁵/₈"	3-10
¾"	4-11
⁷/₈"	6-12
1"	6-14
1¼"	7-16
1½"	6-18
1¾"	8-20
2"	8-20
2¼"	9-20
2½"	12-20
2¾"	14-20
3"	16-20

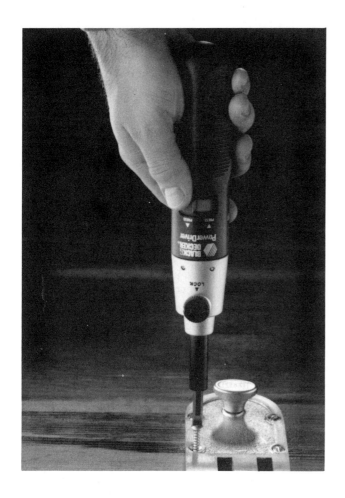

To drive screws easier and straighter, use a power screwdriver with the appropriate tip. Photo courtesy Black & Decker.

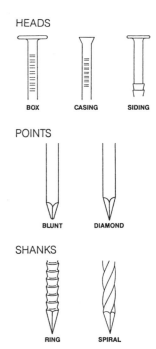

HEADS

BOX   CASING   SIDING

POINTS

BLUNT   DIAMOND

SHANKS

RING   SPIRAL

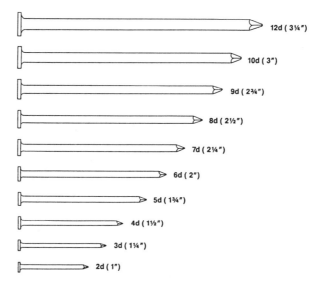

12d (3¼")

10d (3")

9d (2¾")

8d (2½")

7d (2¼")

6d (2")

5d (1¾")

4d (1½")

3d (1¼")

2d (1")

Use corrosion-resistant screws and the go-anywhere cordless drill/driver screw gun for split-free connections on treated lumber. Photo courtesy Black & Decker.

Use a Cyclone Drill/Driver and self-tapping sheet metal screws to make metal-to-metal connections. Photo courtesy Black & Decker.

Cordless Cyclone Drill/Driver has an automatic torque setting that lets you alternate between drilling and screw driving without changing clutch setting. Photo courtesy Black & Decker.

SCREW DIAMETERS

Screw Gauge	Screw Diameter	Pilot Hole Diameter
2	.086	3/64"
3	.099	1/16
4	.112	1/16
5	.125	5/64
6	.138	5/64
7	.151	3/32
8	.164	3/32
9	.177	7/64
10	.190	7/64
11	.203	1/8
12	.216	1/8
13	.229	1/8
14	.242	9/64

NOTE: Screw pilot hole diameters are suggested for hardwood.

BOLTS

Bolts come in a variety of diameters, lengths, and thread counts per inch. Secured with a threaded retaining nut, the threaded bolts provide great strength. Bolts are inserted through pre-drilled holes in the material, and the threaded end is often fitted with a round disc called a washer. The washer, which is usually larger than the nut, reinforces the nut against pullout. The nuts are tightened on the bolts using one of several types of wrenches: adjustable, box, open, and socket wrenches being most common.

Bolts are identified by a set of two numbers. The first number refers to the diameter of the bolt, and the second number refers to the number of threads per inch. For example, a 3/8-16 bolt has a 3/8-inch diameter and 16 threads per inch. Bolts that have a diameter of less than 1/4 inch are assigned numbers: No. 8, No. 10, etc. For example, a bolt might be a 6-32, meaning it is a No. 6 bolt with 32 threads per inch. Metric bolts show both their numbers as mil-limeters: a 10 x 1.25 bolt would be 10 millimeters in diameter, with 1.25 threads per millimeter.

Bolts are used where great fastener strength is required, or for any job where one might want to disassemble the object at a later time. One advantage to using a nut and bolt for holding joists or timbers together is found in the fact that wood shrinks as it dries, and nailed or screwed joints may become loose and shaky. When this happens with a nut-and-bolt assembly, one can tighten the nut to take up the slack from the wood shrinkage.

TIP: To remove a nut from a rusty or corroded bolt, try spraying the bolt threads and nut with a penetrating oil. Wait a few minutes for the penetrating oil to work, then try loosening the nut with a wrench. If this fails, use a propane torch to heat the nut. The nut should expand when heat is applied, making it easier to loosen. For very stubborn cases where the nut simply will not come loose, you can buy a tool called a nutcracker. When you tighten the nutcracker it will split the nut so you can remove it. Then you will have to buy a new nut when reassembling the project. Nutcrackers are available at automotive tool stores.

COST COMPARISON

When planning any project, the price of screws versus nails, or the price of non-corrosive fasteners such as stainless steel or aluminum versus bright steel, may seem to be not worth the cost. Keep in mind that the cost of fasteners, whether nails or screws, is a very small part of the total material cost of most projects. Consider the few dollars you may pay extra for quality fasteners to be a prudent and worthwhile investment to extend the life and the appearance of your project. Think of it this way: you've invested hundreds or perhaps thousands of dollars in lumber for a deck project. Are you willing to see the decking marred by ugly streaks from rust and corrosion of the fasteners? And the next time you see a sagging wood porch, or a barn or house that is sagging out of plumb, chances are good that the structural failures are due to rusting and weakening of the nails that held the project together. Remember the old adage: "For want of a nail, the shoe was lost; for want of a shoe, the horse was lost." Buy the highest quality screws or nails you can find, consistent with the project you are doing.

METAL CONNECTORS

During the economic depression of the 1930s our government was seeking ways to expand the use of all kinds of forest products. This was during the period before technology gave us a widened array of construction adhesives, and before the development of construction screws with their speed of application, via electric screwdrivers, and their superior holding power. Architects and engineers were put to work to find ways to improve the strength of wood joints for residential and commercial construction.

The result of this research was the development of metal connectors for wood. One spinoff result of this connector development was the increased mechanized construction of trusses to speed roof, floor, and wall construction. In an inflationary world, truss construction has helped to hold down on-site construction labor and to make housing affordable. But metal connectors have gone far beyond their acceptance by professional builders. A growing number of metal connectors have become available to the do-it-yourself homeowner. Familiarize yourself with the metal connectors available to you. Keep in mind that toenailing, as mentioned in the section on nails, is not a satisfactory way of achieving a strong wood joint. Toenails tend to split the wood. Also, nailed joints are strongest when the nails are driven in shear, or when the stress or force acts at right angles to the nail. This superior nail technique, where the force is in shear relative to the nail, is the best argument for using metal connectors to join wood.

There are other positive arguments for using metal connectors rather than using nails alone. Framing carpenters often work in pairs, so there are two people to do the job, one to hold each end of a joist or rafter. The homeowner may not have a helper to hold up one end of the joist while he nails the other end in place. Using metal connectors such as joist hangers, one can position and nail in place a pair of joist hangers, then drop the floor or deck joist into the U-shaped cradles formed by the pair of joist hangers. The metal connectors thus serve as a second pair of hands. All that remains is to nail through the connectors to secure the joists.

Your local home center can offer a brochure listing all the different types of metal connectors available for wood projects. There are metal connectors for almost any wood-to-wood connector job. There are flat connectors for joining wood pieces end-to-end or end-to-edge, or for building trusses. Post caps can be used to connect post tops to beams or to joists; post anchor bases connect the bottom of a post to a concrete pier or footing.

All-purpose anchors often can be bent into almost any form to connect wood at odd angles. Metal guard plates can be nailed onto studs or joists at electric wire or water pipe locations, to guard against damage to wires or pipes from nails. Fence brackets can be nailed to the inside edge of fence posts, and the fence rails can be dropped into the brackets. The brackets not only provide an "extra hand" for holding the fence rails in position, you can also leave the rails sitting loose or un-nailed in their brackets, for easy removal. Being able to remove the rails is an advantage when you want to move equipment or material into the yard, or mow grass or shovel snow along and under the fence line.

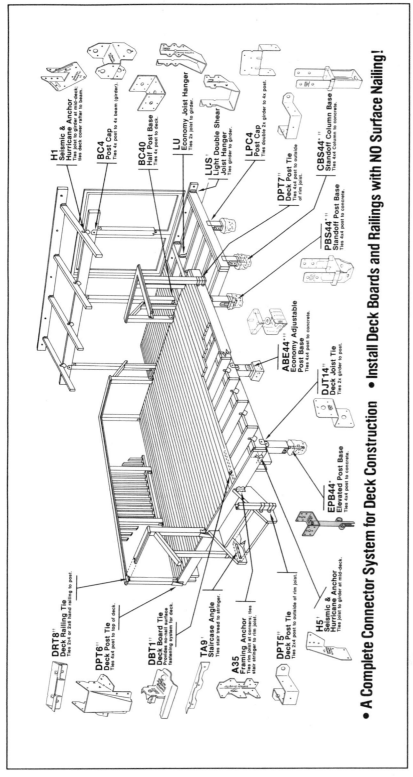

H1
Seismic & Hurricane Anchor
Ties joist to girder at mid-deck; ties deck cover rather to beam.

BC4
Post Cap
Ties 4x post to 4x beam (girder).

BC40
Half Post Base
Ties 4x post to deck.

LU
Economy Joist Hanger
Ties 2x joist to girder.

LUS
Light Double Shear Joist Hanger
Ties girder to girder.

LPC4
Post Cap
Ties double 2x girder to 4x post.

DPT7
Deck Post Tie
Ties 4x4 post to outside of rim joist.

CBS44
Standoff Column Base
Ties 4x4 Column to concrete.

PBS44
Standoff Post Base
Ties 4x4 post to concrete.

ABE44
Economy Adjustable Post Base
Ties 4x4 post to concrete.

DJT14
Deck Joist Tie
Ties 2x girder to post.

EPB44
Elevated Post Base
Ties 4x4 post to concrete.

H5
Seismic & Hurricane Anchor
Ties joist to girder at mid-deck.

DPT5
Deck Post Tie
Ties 4x4 post to outside of rim joist.

A35
Framing Anchor
Ties rim joist at corners; ties stair stringer to rim joist.

TA9
Staircase Angle
Ties stair tread to stringer.

DBT1
Deck Board Tie
Provides no-nail surface fastening system for deck.

DPT6
Deck Post Tie
Ties 4x4 post to top of deck.

DRT8
Deck Railing Tie
Ties 2x4 or 2x6 hand railing to post.

● A Complete Connector System for Deck Construction ● Install Deck Boards and Railings with NO Surface Nailing!

A deck connector system. Courtesy Simpson Strong-Tie® Company, Inc.

Metal connectors are used to build the full-frame truss shown here. Floor, walls, ceiling joists, and roof rafters are connected together in one truss. This speeds construction, results in greater frame strength. Courtesy Forest Products, U.S. Dept. of Agriculture.

To prevent your roof from lifting in a high wind, use tie-down rafter anchors to connect the roof rafters or trusses to the top plate of the walls. Plywood support clips fit over the edges of two sheets of adjoining plywood roof sheathing. The support clips keep the plywood sheathing from sagging between rafters or trusses and also permit you to save lumber by spacing trusses farther apart. Another metal connector that saves lumber and reduces material costs is the backup clip for corners, which replaces wood backing for nailers at corners.

Some metal connectors have speed-nails that are die-punched from the metal itself. You simply drive these projecting speed-nails with the hammer to attach the connector to the wood members to be joined. For other metal connectors that do not have speed-nails, use ordinary nails to attach the connectors to wood. Use galvanized nails to install metal connectors where they will be exposed to the weather. To prevent future corrosion and wood stains, use a metal-type aerosol paint to spray paint the metal connectors before you install them.

STAPLES

Staples are available that can be driven with a hammer, (e.g. fence staples), or by using a staple gun. You'll find a staple gun, either spring-driven or electric, to be a useful addition to your tool chest. The staple gun should be able to use a variety of staple lengths, from ¼ inch up to ½ inch at least, to perform a wide range of tasks. A staple gun can be used to install faced batt insulation; for installing a plastic sheet vapor barrier on ceilings or outside walls; to install new wire on wood window screens; to staple ceiling tile; and for carpet and furniture upholstery repairs.

RIVETS

Rivets are commonly used to join two pieces of sheet metal, or to join (using backup plates) canvas or leather items together. Tubular copper rivets can be hand applied. Just drill a hole for the rivet, insert the proper length rivet, and place a backup plate over the end. Then lay the rivet over a hard surface, such as the face of a vise or anvil, and flatten or "peen" the rivet over, using a ball-peen hammer.

A more common rivet is the blind or "Pop" rivet, which is flattened using a rivet gun. (Pop Brand Rivetool is a trademarked name of Bostik.) The most common rivet diameter is $1/8$ inch, although larger rivet guns and rivets are available.

To use the blind rivet gun, drill a rivet hole the same diameter as the rivet—usually $1/8$ inch. If the rivet hole in the sheet metal is rough, use a somewhat larger bit as a deburring tool to smooth the rough edges of the hole. Just insert the oversized bit tip into the hole and turn it by hand to remove any burrs from the edges of the rivet hole.

Then insert a rivet of the proper length in the rivet hole. Depending on the strength needed for the repair you may want to make, you may want to use a backup plate (small washer) over the back side of the rivet. Place the shaft of the rivet in the hole in the end of the rivet gun, and squeeze the handles of the gun to flatten the back side of the rivet and to break off the rivet shaft.

To remove the rivet or to take the assembly apart, carefully drill through the rivet head using a bit the same diameter as the rivet shank (again, usually a $1/8$-inch bit). Drill slowly through the head, and the head should pop off the rivet shank. Drill or punch out the rivet shank to complete the rivet removal.

TIP for metal drilling: To make a starter hole and to prevent the bit from drifting across the workpiece, use a sharp punch to start a dent. Then use a slow speed on your variable-speed drill to drill the hole through metal.

4.
Lumber

If you intend to become a dedicated do-it-yourself-er, you should take the time to study and understand the markings on lumber and plywood. The success of any building project depends on choosing the right materials to use. Lumber and plywood are marked to provide you with important information about the intended end use of the wood. By understanding lumber markings you can be sure you are using the best and most economical grade of lumber for your project, so you will get the best results while saving money by not buying material that is a better grade than you need.

SPECIES

Lumber is identified according to the species of tree from which it is produced, i.e., redwood, spruce, pine, oak, etc. It is further divided into softwoods and hardwoods. These terms do not refer to the actual hardness or density of the particular lumber. By definition, softwoods come from trees that have needles, such as pine or fir; hardwoods come from trees that have leaves, such as oak or maple.

GRADE

Lumber is further identified according to grade. Characteristics such as appearance, grain direction and density, natural and manufacturing defects, and strength are taken into account in grading the lumber. Lumber is sight-graded (visually) board by board by inspectors at the lumber mills, who separate and stamp the lumber according to its particular characteristics of strength and appearance.

MOISTURE CONTENT

Lumber is also identified according to its moisture content. For example, a fresh-cut tree may have a 50 percent moisture content. This moisture will be lost naturally as the lumber is milled and dries out, but moisture loss is accelerated by the mill by the use of lumber dryers or kilns. Wet lumber that has a high moisture content is unsuitable for building, because it will shrink, warp, and split as it dries out, so it is important to reduce the moisture content before using the wood in building projects. This step ensures that the lumber will not shrink or warp

Southern pine, the species most often used for pressure-treated lumber, is a fast-growing resource. Photo courtesy Hickson Corp.

Take normal precautions when working with treated lumber: wear gloves and eye goggles, wash hands after handling the wood. Photo courtesy Hickson Corp.

Custom millwork products made with pressure-treated wood allow you full design freedom. Photo courtesy Weyerhauser.

Wood shown is Wolmanized Extra™, which is treated with water repellent in addition to preservatives. Photo courtesy Hickson Corp.

Pressure-treated lumber has proven its safety for people, pets, and plants, in more than fifty-five years of use. Photo courtesy Hickson Corp.

too much after the house, furniture, or other project is finished.

In addition to warping and shrinking, high moisture content in lumber can also result in rusted or corroded fasteners, and cracking, flaking, or peeling of any paint or finish coat. Choose lumber that is low in moisture content to ensure getting the best results.

When wood moisture content has been reduced to 15 percent, usually the level that is referred to as "kiln-dried," the wood has undergone about one-half its potential shrinkage. To be useful, dimension lumber must be stamped S-DRY (Surface-dry), meaning it has a moisture content of 19 percent or less. Lumber that is stamped GRN (green) has a moisture content over 19 percent. Carpenters often joke of GRN lumber that you first have to pick the leaves off it before you can begin nailing.

Many people misunderstand the term "settle," as in "the house will crack as it settles." The term does not mean that the footings will sink away; *settling* is the term used to refer to the materials in the house losing moisture and shrinking, which often results in cracks in the walls or gaps in the wood trim. Projects built with green or wet lumber will literally pull themselves apart as the wood loses moisture and shrinks.

Kiln-dried lumber has a moisture content of 15 percent or less, which ensures that framing done with this lumber will stay straight and strong, without excessive shrinkage or warping.

Because it also serves for decorative and ornamental purposes and will be in view throughout the life of the building, finish lumber used for trim, moldings, cabinetry, flooring, and furniture should have an even lower moisture content than framing lumber. Interior trim and flooring lumber should have a moisture content between 7 percent and 10 percent.

Lumber moisture content is critical to the success of a building project; this point cannot be emphasized too strongly. Many builders and cabinet makers who are considered master craftsmen owe much of their reputation for quality to their ability to choose superior materials for the job.

LUMBER GRADES

GRADE	DESCRIPTION/USES
SEL STR or select structural 1, 2, 3	Clear or small, tight knots, with good strength and stiffness. Grades 1, 2, 3 refer to knot size.
CONST or Construction STAND or Standard	Both CONST and STAND grades have good strength and are used in trusses and general framing applications.
STUD or Stud	Used for any stud application, including load-bearing walls.
UTIL or Utility	Used for blocking, bracing, building concrete forms, or other applications where appearance is not critical.
NOTE: Buy lumber where you can perform your own inspection for knots, splits, and warping of the wood, and hand-pick your materials.	

BOARD MEASURE

For Board (1") Lumber

Nominal Size	Actual Size	Board Feet/ Linear Feet
1 x 2	³⁄₄ x 1½	¹⁄₆ (.167)
1 x 3	³⁄₄ x 2½	¼ (.250)
1 x 4	³⁄₄ x 3½	¹⁄₃ (.333)
1 x 6	³⁄₄ x 5½	½ (.500)
1 x 8	³⁄₄ x 7¼	²⁄₃ (.666)
1 x 10	³⁄₄ x 9¼	⁵⁄₆ (.833)
1 x 12	³⁄₄ x 11¼	1 (1.0)

For Dimensional (2") Lumber

Nominal Size	Actual Size	Board Feet/ Linear Feet
2 x 2	1½ x 1½	¹⁄₃ (.333)
2 x 3	1½ x 2½	½ (.500)
2 x 4	1½ x 3½	²⁄₃ (.666)
2 x 6	1½ x 5½	1 (1.0)
2 x 8	1½ x 7¼	1¹⁄₃ (1.333)
2 x 10	1½ x 9¼	1 ²⁄₃ (1.666)
2 x 12	1½ x 11¼	2 (2.0)

HEADER SPAN GUIDE

Size Lumber (Double)	Span
2 x 4	3'-0"
2 x 6	5'-0"
2 x 8	7'-0"
2 x 10	8'-0"
2 x 12	9'-0"

Note: Dimensional lumber is 1½" thick. To make a header that is 2 x 4 width (3½"), cut a piece of ½" thick plywood to the length and width of the framing lumber needed, and sandwich the ½" thick plywood between two framing members. For example: To make a 5' long window header, cut a piece of ½" thick plywood, 5' long x 5½" wide. Cut two 5' long 2 x 6s. Place the plywood between the 2 x 6s and nail the three pieces together.

DRYING LUMBER

In addition to checking the lumber markings for moisture content before buying, you can also take other steps to be sure that lumber and other wood products have a stable moisture content, i.e., that they are dry enough to use, after they are delivered.

Lumber mills often wax the ends of framing lumber to prevent the lumber from absorbing airborne humidity or moisture. Still, lumber that is warehoused outdoors or in unheated lumber sheds can pick up moisture from the air during humid weather. For building projects such as applying trim, or for cabinet or furniture building, buy your material from a supplier that has an indoor warehouse where temperature and humidity are controlled. Find a lumber yard or home center that caters to professional carpenters to be sure you are getting quality wood materials.

Next, buy wood products for your projects well ahead of schedule, and store them in the area where they will be used. At room temperatures and normal moisture levels the wood products will quickly acclimate, meaning they will reach a moisture content level to match their environment. Conditioning building materials for even a few days can make a difference in how the wood products perform in place.

Treated Lumber—Moisture

The moisture content found in pressure-treated lumber is an entirely different matter from that of untreated lumber. With pressure- or chemically-treated lumber, fluids are injected under pressure into the wood fiber, so the moisture content is often still quite high when you buy the material. The best procedure here is to buy the material where you can hand-pick the lumber for general condition and freedom from warping or splitting.

Having picked lumber that is straight, stack your pressure-treated material at home for drying. This can be done by placing spacers such as wood lath between the pieces of lumber, so that air can circulate through the stack and reach every board. This drying can be a lengthy process if the material is very wet. I once left pressure-treated deck lumber to dry in the sun for three weeks of 90° weather before using it. Even so, the lumber showed quite a degree of shrinkage after it had weathered in place. Also, do not be in a hurry to apply stain or paint to your project—wet lumber does not accept finishes well. For outdoor projects, buy pressure-treated lumber that has also been protected (by the manufacturer) with a sealer, and don't attempt to stain or finish it until it has aged and dried for a season.

WOOD FOR WEATHER

Wood is a renewable, lightweight, inexpensive, and durable building material. If any wood is properly protected from the ravages of weather and pests it will last virtually forever. However, some species of wood, such as redwood, cedar, and cypress, are naturally more resistant to damage from the elements than other species. Keep in mind that the heartwood is the most durable part of these species.

Also, technology via chemistry has found ways to treat almost all species of wood to make them more durable and resistant to moisture or insect damage. For any wood project that will be exposed to weather, moisture, or insect attack, choose from among the more durable wood building materials.

TREATED LUMBER

We have long known that injecting chemicals such as CCA (chromated copper arsenate) into wood at extremely high pressures could yield a wood product that would have greatly enhanced resistance to attack from weather and insects. Sea walls, docks, and piers made from treated lumber and continuously exposed to salt seawater have stood for decades. Use of treated lumber was once restricted to commercial and industrial applications, but twenty years ago manufacturers of treated wood got into the consumer product market.

One result of developing pressure-treated lumber products has been to take the pressure off the harvest of some of the naturally-resistant species such as redwood and cedar. Species such as Southern pine can be injected with chemical protectants to give them longer life, and these fast-growing trees mature so quickly that they are truly a renewable resource.

The durability of the treated lumber depends on the amount of chemical injected into the wood. The lumber will have markings indicating whether it is intended for ground contact, such as posts, or whether it is suited only for above-ground application, such as for fencing or decking. If you're not sure which product to buy, ask the store clerk to advise you to be sure you get the right product for your particular job.

Treated lumber is resistant to damage from water or insects. But, because treated lumber can be produced from wood species that have an open wood grain, it can sometimes suffer splitting and cracking if it is not further protected from moisture. A number of wood treatment products have been developed to address this problem on existing decks or other structures, and manufacturers now offer treated lumber that is also protected with a sealer. One such product is Wolmanized Extra™, which received great buyer acceptance when it was introduced in 1990.

The growth in treated lumber sales has seen a parallel growth in manufacture of ancillary wood products. Treated lattice and plywood are now offered. Custom turned treated wood products such as posts, rails, balusters, and finials are offered under the name Weyerhauser LifeWood, among others.

Treated Lumber: How Safe?

The Environmental Protection Agency (EPA) has tested pressure-treated lumber and found it to be safe for any ordinary home project application. There are some common-sense precautions that you should take when using pressure-treated wood, but manufacturers point out that these precautions should be observed when handling *any* wood products, whether natural or chemically treated.

- You should not use pressure-treated wood for countertops where food may be prepared, but the U.S. Food and Drug Administration does not recommend using *any* wood for a food-cutting surface, because particles of food may become embedded in the wood surface and cause unsanitary conditions.

- Wear a dust mask to avoid inhaling sawdust or other particles as you saw, sand, or drill any wood product. Wear goggles to protect eyes from flying splinters or chips.

- Wear gloves when handling any wood to protect your hands from splinters. Leather gloves are toughest and offer the best protection against sharp splinters.

- Wash hands after work and before eating, drinking, or smoking, regardless of what material you are handling.

- The EPA has approved pressure-treated lumber as a safe play surface for children.

Many schools and parks are now using treated lumber for building playground equipment.

- Treated lumber may be used indoors where extra protection is needed. Treated lumber does not give off any fumes or vapors when used indoors.

- Dispose of treated lumber in an approved landfill. Do not burn scrap lumber in your fireplace. The resulting smoke and ash may be toxic.

TIP: When building decks with treated lumber, use PL500 Deck and Treated Lumber Adhesive to secure deck boards to joists. The adhesive will eliminate splintering and nail pops that are common with nailed decking lumber.

All-Weather Wood Foundations

A frequent consumer question on our talk radio shows concerns the advisability of using wood foundations, rather than using the more familiar concrete foundation construction. Treated lumber has been used for foundations for several decades, but industry acceptance of the practice was slow in developing. It was difficult for both builders and consumers to accept that wood buried in the earth would not quickly decay. But while working as an editor of a housing magazine some years ago I received information on a wood house foundation, located in Wisconsin, that was more than thirty years old. The foundation was dug up and inspected, and was found to have survived the thirty years without any damage from moisture or insects.

Wood foundations can be used either for houses with crawl space or full basement construction. The key to success in using wood foundations is proper drainage around the wood footings, (to wrap the foundation walls in protective polyethylene plastic film), and to build foundation walls using treated lumber that is suitable for ground contact.

Building wood foundations is a job that is best left to professionals who have experience in the work. The basic procedure is to dig and level the trenches for the footings. Several inches of gravel, sand, or crushed rock are placed in the footing excavations, then the gravel or other material is leveled and tamped. Use a treated 2 x 12 as a footing, and nail it to the bottom plate of the foundation wall.

The all-wood foundation wall is framed just like an above-ground wall, except treated lumber is used in construction. The studs used are treated 2 x 6s, or larger, depending on the type of soil, the width of the house, and whether it is one or two stories high. The framed wall is covered with treated plywood, the thickness of which again will depend on the loads the walls will carry and the type of soil. After the plywood is in place, the entire wood foundation (exterior) is wrapped with a polyethylene plastic film to help keep the structure dry. On a full wood basement wall the concrete floor is poured on the inside, to prevent the bottom of the wall from tipping in, and the exterior side of the wall is backfilled with gravel and earth, then graded to ensure that water runs away from the house. If the wood wall is a foundation for a crawl space and is not full basement height, the wall is stabilized with earth backfill from both interior and exterior sides.

The wood foundation system is usually cheaper than a poured concrete or concrete block foundation. The wood foundation can be built in a factory and hauled to its location for installation, which is a definite plus for construction in cold climates where pouring concrete in winter is difficult. In place, the wood foundation is warmer than concrete and has stud cavities that can be filled with fiberglass batt insulation. The wood construction makes the basement easier for the do-it-yourselfer to finish, because concrete basement walls are more difficult for the homeowner to finish himself.

For more information about the all-weather wood foundation system, contact the National Forest Products Association, 1619 Massachusetts Avenue N.W., Washington, DC 20036.

REDWOOD

Redwood has natural qualities that make it an excellent choice for either exterior or interior projects. The close grain and natural resistance to damage from either decay or insects mean that projects built of redwood will hold their value and age beautifully. Redwood also takes and holds a protective finish—paint or stain—better than many other wood species. Use redwood for siding, decks, fences, or other exterior applications where both beauty and durability are required. Although redwood can seem a bit expensive, the consumer can stay within the budget by being sure to specify the correct material choice for the job. For example, only the wood that will be in ground contact needs to be the most expensive heart lumber; cheaper grades can be used for above-ground applications. Specifications should include: use, grade, grain, seasoning, size, and texture information. Your lumber dealer can help you choose the best grades for each particular part of your project.

There are more than thirty grades of redwood lumber. A primary factor in grading redwood is appearance and color. Reddish-brown heartwood contains extractives that protect it against decay and insect attack. The lighter, cream-colored sapwood that grows in the outer layer of the trees does not have the natural protective characteristics of heartwood.

Other grades are determined by the size and number of knots and the presence of stains or manufacturing defects. The grades are:

Architectural grades: Clear All Heart, Clear, and B Grade are all kiln dried for the premium interior or

Performance Characteristics of Construction Woods	Total Performance	Freedom from Shrinking	Freedom from Warping	Decay Resistance (Heartwood)	Paint Holding	Freedom from Pitch (Resin)	Workability	Nail Holding	Bending Strength	Stiffness	Hardness
California redwood	26	3	3	3	3	3	3	2	2	2	2
Douglas fir-larch	23	2	2	2	1	2	2	3	3	3	3
Western cedar	22	3	3	3	3	3	3	1	1	1	1
Southern pine	22	2	2	2	1	1	2	3	3	3	3
Eastern hemlock	21	3	2	1	2	3	2	2	2	2	2
Hem-fir	19	2	2	1	1	3	2	2	2	2	2
Idaho white pine	19	2	3	1	3	3	3	1	1	1	1
Spruce-pine-fir (Canada)	17	2	2	1	1	3	1	2	2	2	1
Englemann spruce-lodgepole pine	15	2	2	1	1	3	2	1	1	1	1

3 Among woods relatively high in the characteristic listed.

2 Among woods intermediate in that respect.

1 Among woods relatively low in that respect.

Rankings of species taken from:
How to Buy Construction Lumber
University of Wisconsin-Extension/Madison
September 1979

Redwood siding patterns. Courtesy California Redwood Association

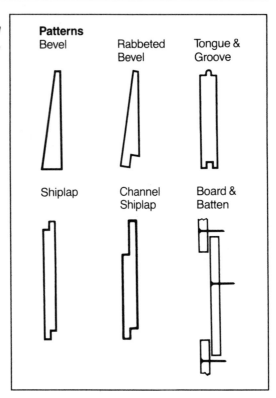

Patterns

Bevel

Rabbeted Bevel

Tongue & Groove

Shiplap

Channel Shiplap

Board & Batten

Redwood—Architectural Grades: (Left to right) Clear All Heart, Clear, and B Grade Redwood are the finest kiln-dried finish grades and are used for siding, cabinetry, and trim where beauty and fit are desired. Courtesy California Redwood Association.

*Redwood—Garden Grades: Construction Heart (left) and Construction Common (right)
Redwoods are used for decks or other structures where knots or other characteristics have
little effect. Use Construction Heart for ground level, Construction Common for above ground
applications. Courtesy California Redwood Association.*

exterior applications. These architectural grades are the choice grades for siding, paneling, trim, and cabinetry.

Garden grades: Construction Heart, Construction Common, Merchantable Heart, and Merchantable grades may be specified for use where knots or color variations are not important. Decks, fences, and other garden projects are typical uses for the garden grades.

For projects where the wood will be in or near ground contact, such as posts or patio grids, use one of the heartwood grades such as Clear All Heart, Select Heart, Construction Heart, or Merchantable Heart.

For projects where the wood will not be in ground contact, one of the less expensive sapwood-containing grades will serve as well and at the same time will help you stay within the budget. These grades are Clear, B Grade, Select, Construction Common, and Merchantable.

Characteristics of Redwood

A very important characteristic of redwood is its

stability, or resistance to shrinking. In fact, tests by the U.S. Forest Products Association show that redwood has the least volumetric shrinkage of any commercial American wood. The tests showed that from its green condition to a 10 percent moisture content, redwood shrinks only 1.7 percent across the vertical grain and only 3.3 percent across the flat grain. This resistance to shrinkage plays an important role in the quality of the finished project. As mentioned earlier, lumber that shrinks excessively will cause your project to have loose joints, popping nails or other fasteners, structural sagging, and premature failure.

We have already talked about redwood's durability, its natural resistance to decay and to insect infestation. Natural extractives in the heartwood provide high resistance to termite attack and make redwood one of only two untreated woods approved for use as foundation plates or "mudsills" by the Uniform Building Code.

The closed grain and resistance to shrinking make redwood easy to glue. To have superior gluing qualities, the strength of the glued joint should be equal to the strength of the wood itself. Redwoods perform well with glues and adhesives. Also, the texture and grain patterns of redwood make it easy to work with a plane, joiner, or router.

Other positive characteristics of redwood include a good strength-to-weight ratio: redwood is one of the lightest softwoods used for structural purposes. It has good nail-holding power and, because it has no volatile resins or oils, good fire resistance. For further information on redwood, contact the California Redwood Association at (415) 382-0662.

CEDAR

Cedar is another wood that has good appearance plus a natural resistance to decay and insect attack. Cedar has many of the same qualities as redwood. Left natural, it will gray down with age and will yield a long service life. Cedar is often used for siding, and became very popular during the '60s when used in its rustic "rough-sawn" look. Western cedar long ago proved its durability as the species of choice for fence posts on farms or ranches.

The natural light brown or tan color of cedar makes it a natural choice for the all-cedar homes manufactured on the West Coast. Like redwood, cedar is at home either on the interior or the exterior of the house, and is a low-maintenance material favorite both for primary homes and for vacation home retreats.

Those same attributes—attractive appearance, durability, and low maintenance—have made cedar one of the "big three" material choices for building outdoor structures. Consider cedar when planning a deck, gazebo, or fence, or when re-siding your house. For more information contact: Western Wood Products Association at (503) 224-3930.

OUTDOOR WOOD: HOW TO CHOOSE?

So you're planning to add a deck or build a gazebo, and you must choose which lumber to use. How can you choose between treated lumber, redwood, and cedar?

If your choice is guided by initial price alone, you will probably find that treated lumber is the least expensive wood choice. If you are trying to blend your project's appearance with existing siding or with other nearby yard structures, you may want to conform and build to match the surroundings, whatever the prior wood choices. Or you may simply prefer the appearance of either redwood or cedar, and cost may be a secondary consideration.

One trick pro carpenters have used is to use less expensive treated lumber for the deck framing or superstructure—posts, beams, and joists. Then they switch to cedar or redwood for the "appearance" part of the deck: the deck boards, railings, built-in benches, and stairs.

Only you can decide which material you will use. Whatever your choice, observe good building procedure to ensure long life and low maintenance for your project. If you place the deck posts in holes, cover the bottom of the hole with gravel to provide good drainage and to prevent premature rot of the wood. Or pour concrete support piers and use metal post base connectors to tie the wood posts to the concrete piers. The metal connectors hold the bottom end of the post slightly above the concrete so that water can drain away from the end of the post. The post will stay dry and not rot if air can circulate around it.

Follow the manufacturer's advice, or material dealer's brochures, when building any project. The manufacturer(s) want you to be happy with your product choice, and they provide instructional information to help you get the most out of their products. An informational point that may seem trivial to you in fact may be very important: the manufacturer is trying to give you the benefit of his experience and to help you avoid construction pitfalls. Read and heed instructions.

For example: One bit of advice that is often ignored is to use corrosion-resistant fasteners when building outdoor projects. How do we know this tip is ignored? Check the black or rust-colored streaks around the nail heads on natural wood siding, or on most deck or fence projects. Those black streaks are avoidable simply by using hot dipped galvanized or stainless steel nails. If you want to see just how cheap stainless steel nails are, call your local painter and ask him the cost of removing the nail stains from the deck or siding where stainless steel nails were not used. Keep in mind the old axiom: the quality and beauty of the project will be remembered long after the cost is forgotten.

Another point to remember is to build your deck so it will drain and dry quickly after a rain. If you've seen the top rail on a deck that is built with a slight slope, that is done to ensure good drainage so the lumber will not hold moisture and rot. The advice to position deck boards with the "bark side" or growth rings up is intended to help prevent the deck boards from cupping and holding water.

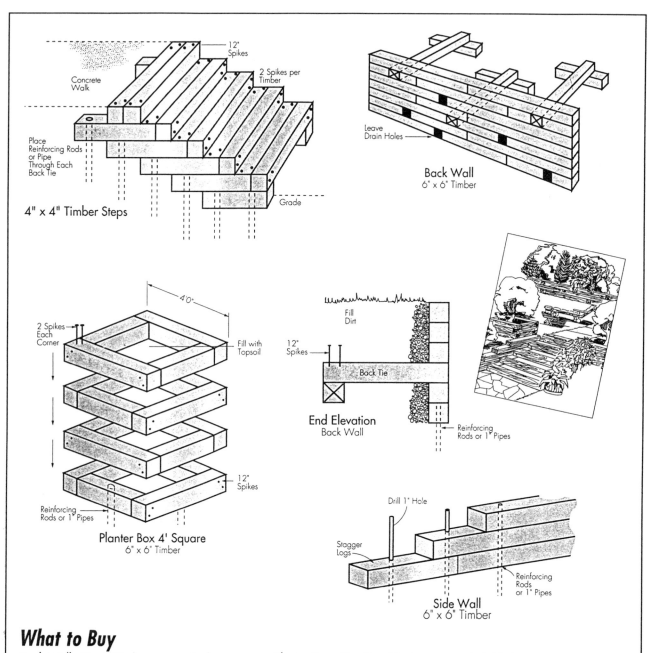

What to Buy

Back Wall: 6" x 6" Timbers as required
Steps: 4" x 4" Timbers as required. Length will depend on width of Steps desired. Number of Steps to be determinmed by size of slope.
Side Wall: Staggered as shown. Use 6" x 6" Timbers as needed, 6' lengths.

Planter Box: 6" x 6" x 4'Timbers as needed. Nail together in 4' squares and attach to Wall Steps.
Hardware: 12" Hot-dipped Galvanized Spikes as needed. 1" Reinforcing Rods or 1" Pipe, 3' lengths. Use 1 Rod/Pipe for each Back Tie.

Landscape wall and steps. Courtesy of Hickson Corp.

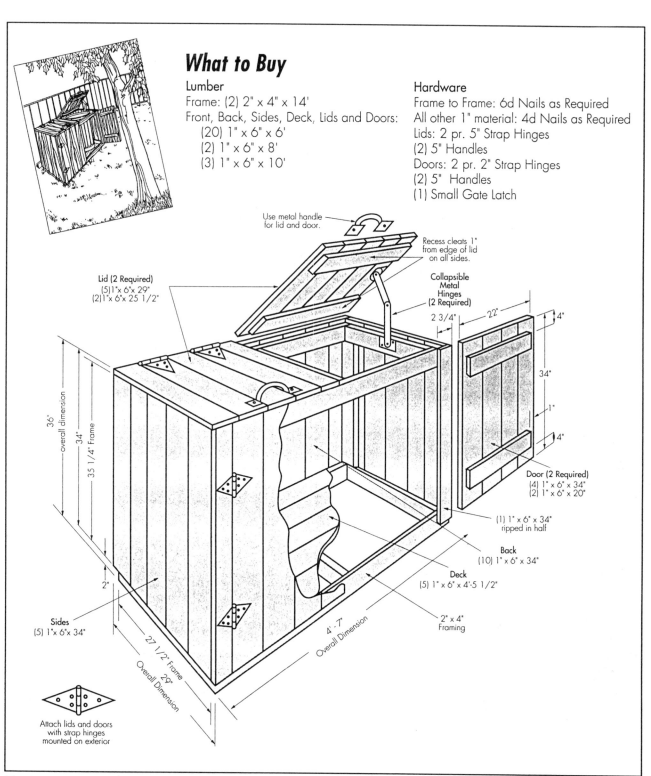

What to Buy

Lumber
Frame: (2) 2" x 4" x 14'
Front, Back, Sides, Deck, Lids and Doors:
(20) 1" x 6" x 6'
(2) 1" x 6" x 8'
(3) 1" x 6" x 10'

Hardware
Frame to Frame: 6d Nails as Required
All other 1" material: 4d Nails as Required
Lids: 2 pr. 5" Strap Hinges
(2) 5" Handles
Doors: 2 pr. 2" Strap Hinges
(2) 5" Handles
(1) Small Gate Latch

Use metal handle
for lid and door.

Recess cleats 1"
from edge of lid
on all sides.

Lid (2 Required)
(5) 1" x 6" x 29"
(2) 1" x 6" x 25 1/2"

Collapsible
Metal
Hinges
(2 Required)

2 3/4"

22"

4"

34"

1"

4"

Door (2 Required)
(4) 1" x 6" x 34"
(2) 1" x 6" x 20"

(1) 1" x 6" x 34"
ripped in half

Back
(10) 1" x 6" x 34"

Deck
(5) 1" x 6" x 4'-5 1/2"

2" x 4"
Framing

36"
overall dimension

34"

35 1/4" Frame

2"

Sides
(5) 1" x 6" x 34"

27 1/2" Frame

29"
Overall Dimension

4' - 7"
Overall Dimension

Attach lids and doors
with strap hinges
mounted on exterior

Trash can bin. Courtesy of Hickson Corp.

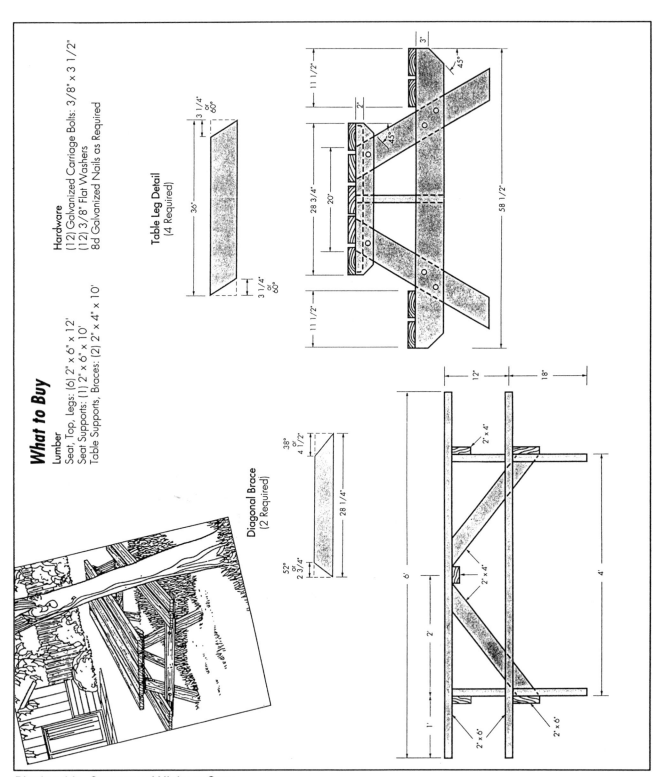

Picnic table. Courtesy of Hickson Corp.

What to Buy

Lumber
Seat, Top, Legs: (6) 2" x 6" x 12'
Seat Supports: (1) 2" x 6" x 10'
Table Supports, Braces: (2) 2" x 4" x 10'

Hardware
(12) Galvanized Carriage Bolts: 3/8" x 3 1/2"
(12) 3/8" Flat Washers
8d Galvanized Nails as Required

Table Leg Detail
(4 Required)

3 1/4"
or
60°

36"

3 1/4"
or
60°

Diagonal Brace
(2 Required)

38°
or
4 1/2"

52°
or
2 3/4"

28 1/4"

3'
45°

11 1/2"

2"

45°

28 3/4"
20"

58 1/2"

11 1/2"

12'

18'

2' x 4'

2' x 4'

6'

2'

4'

1'

2' x 6'

2' x 6'

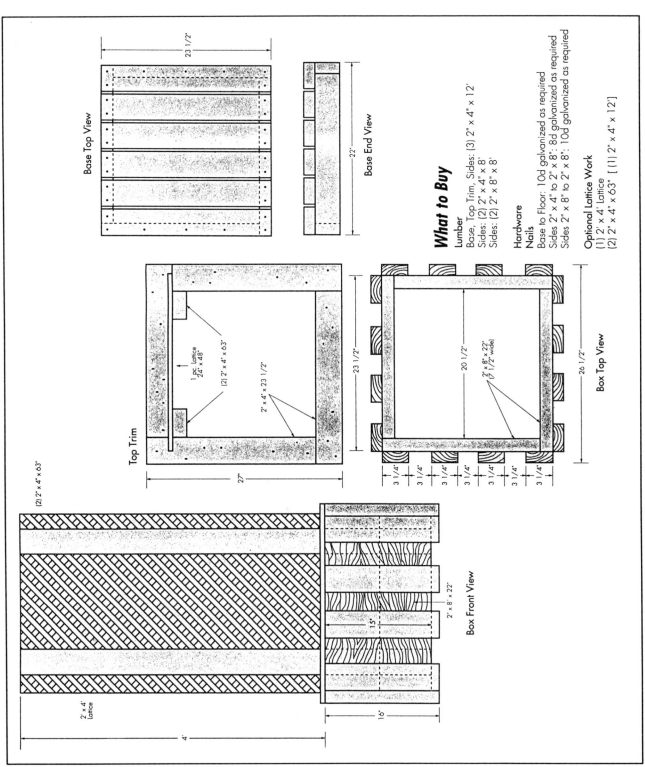

Base Top View

23 1/2"

Base End View

22'

What to Buy

Lumber
Base, Top Trim, Sides: (3) 2" x 4" x 12'
Sides: (2) 2" x 4" x 8'
Sides: (2) 2" x 8" x 8'

Hardware
Nails
Base to Floor: 10d galvanized as required
Sides 2" x 4" to 2" x 8": 8d galvanized as required
Sides 2" x 8' to 2" x 8": 10d galvanized as required

Optional Lattice Work
(1) 2 x 4' Lattice
(2) 2" x 4" x 63" [(1) 2" x 4" x 12']

Top Trim

1 pc. Lattice 24" x 48"

(2) 2" x 4" x 63"

2" x 4" x 23 1/2"

23 1/2'

27'

Box Top View

20 1/2"

2" x 8" x 22"
(7 1/2" wide)

26 1/2"

3 1/4" 3 1/4" 3 1/4" 3 1/4" 3 1/4" 3 1/4" 3 1/4"

(2) 2" x 4" x 63"

2" x 4' Lattice

4'

Box Front View

2" x 8" x 22'

15"

16'

Planter box. Courtesy of Hickson Corp.

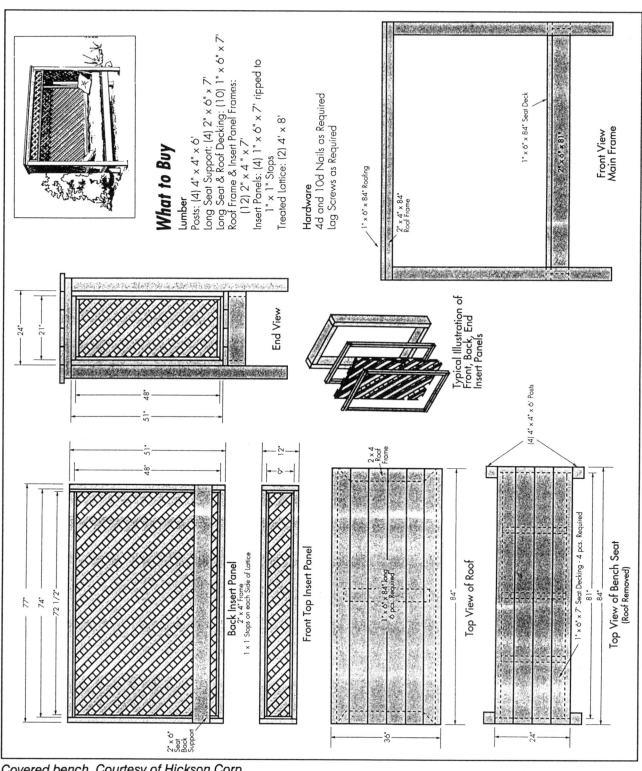

What to Buy

Lumber
Posts: (4) 4" x 4" x 6'
Long Seat Support: (4) 2" x 6" x 7'
Long Seat & Roof Decking: (10) 1" x 6" x 7'
Roof Frame & Insert Panel Frames:
(12) 2" x 4" x 7'
Insert Panels: (4) 1" x 6" x 7' ripped to
1" x 1" Stops
Treated Lattice: (2) 4' x 8'

Hardware
4d and 10d Nails as Required
Lag Screws as Required

1" x 6" x 84" Roofing

2" x 4" x 84" Roof Frame

1" x 6" x 84" Seat Deck

2" x 6" x 81"

Front View Main Frame

24"

21"

48"

51"

End View

Typical Illustration of Front, Back, End Insert Panels

77"

74"

72 1/2"

51"

48"

Back Insert Panel
2" x 4" Frame
1 x 1 Stops on each Side of Lattice

2" x 6" Seat Back Support

12"

9"

Front Top Insert Panel

2 x 4 Roof Frame

1" x 6' x 84" long 6 pcs. Required

36"

84"

Top View of Roof

(4) 4" x 4" x 6' Posts

1" x 6" x 7' Seat Decking - 4 pcs. Required

81"

84"

24"

Top View of Bench Seat
(Roof Removed)

Covered bench. Courtesy of Hickson Corp.

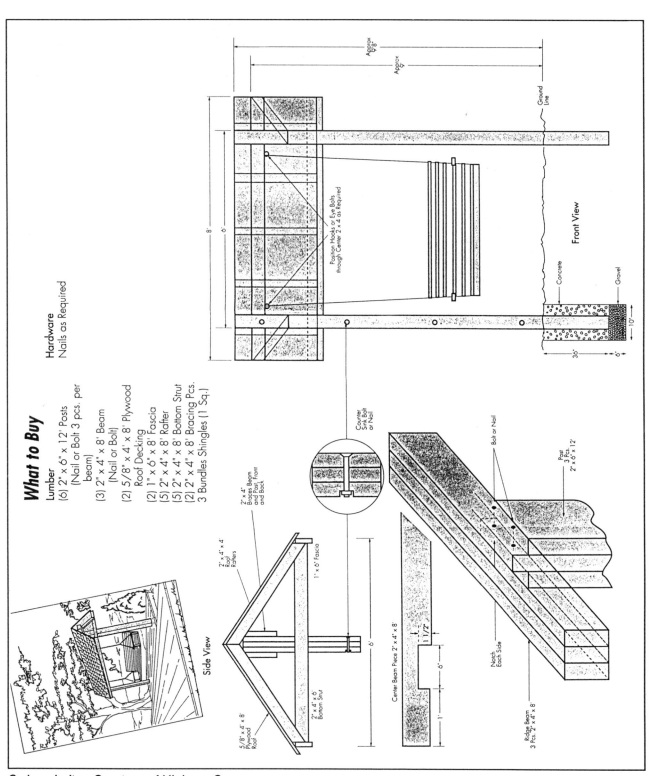

What to Buy

Lumber

(6) 2" x 6" x 12' Posts (Nail or Bolt 3 pcs. per beam)

(3) 2" x 4" x 8' Beam (Nail or Bolt)

(2) 5/8" x 4' x 8' Plywood Roof Decking

(2) 1" x 6" x 8' Fascia

(5) 2" x 4" x 8' Rafter

(5) 2" x 4" x 8' Bottom Strut

(2) 2" x 4" x 8' Bracing Pcs.

3 Bundles Shingles (1 Sq.)

Hardware

Nails as Required

Swing shelter. Courtesy of Hickson Corp.

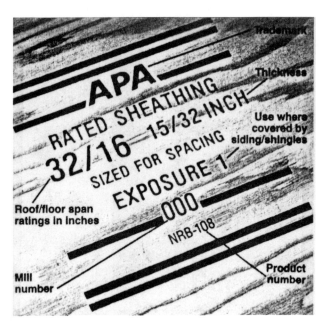

Sheathing plywood grading stamp shows thickness, roof or floor span index, and exposure rating.

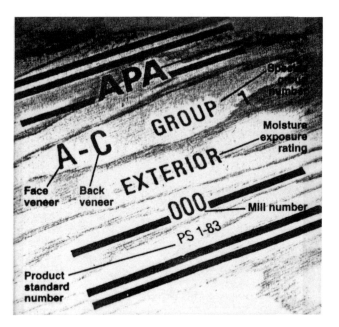

The finished plywood grading stamp shows the trademark, thickness, spacing interval, mill and product number (for manufacturer's use).

5.
Sheet Materials

The term "sheet materials" refers to any material that comes in sheet form, usually 4 feet wide by 6, 8, 10, or 12 feet long. This category includes wood products such as particle board, wafer board, hardboard, plywood, and paneling. It also includes wallboard and cement boards such as Durock™, a United States Gypsum product used on interior or exterior applications as a base for ceramic tile or for stucco. In this chapter we'll give you a brief roundup of tips on what to consider when you are buying any of these sheet materials.

PARTICLE BOARD

The development of improved-strength chemical adhesives has helped the lumber industry utilize materials that once were discarded as wood waste. Particle board is one of those waste byproducts that uses sawdust and small wood particles, combined with adhesives and formed into sheets of uniform thickness, using high pressures and temperatures. The resulting product, called particle board, can be used in houses as underlayment

(under carpet only—particle board should not be used as a base for installing vinyl or ceramic floor covering). Particle board is also used for cabinet countertops, for partitions between cabinets and drawers, for closet and other shelving, and for furniture applications. Particle board is used as a base for door jambs and other trim, where a ply or veneer of hardwood is glued over the particle board base.

Particle board and other manufactured board products help us to utilize and conserve our forest products and also help hold down the rising cost of construction and furniture items. Because of its construction, particle board is not suited for use on outdoor projects or anywhere that high humidity or moisture levels are present. If you install laminate countertops that have a particle board base, you should apply a coat of paint or wood sealer around the edges of the particle board, where you make the sink cutout. Sealing the edge of the sink cutout will prevent moisture from penetrating into the particle board and causing a degradation or glue failure between the particle board and the plastic laminate material (such as Formica®). Particle board is available in a choice of thicknesses (½-inch thick being most common), depending on its intended use or application.

WAFER/ORIENTED STRAND BOARD

Both of these products are made from wood fibers that are mixed with resins and formed into sheets. Both of these products enable the forest industry to utilize less desirable or less mature wood species to manufacture building materials. Wafer board is made by slicing soft wood into wafers that resemble potato chips in size and shape. These wafers are then mixed with resins and formed into sheet materials that can be used for most of the same applications as plywood. Because the wood wafers are completely wrapped up or encapsulated in the resin, the wafer board can be used for both interior and exterior applications.

Rather than slicing wood into wafers, as is done with wafer board, oriented strand board is made by separating wood fibers and then bonding them together with resins into sheets. Like wafer board, strand board enables us to use lesser species of wood to manufacture building material. Fast-growing wood species of trees such as poplar, which would not otherwise be commercially utilized, can not only be used but their rapid growth also means they are truly a renewable forest resource.

HARDBOARD

Hardboard, like the sheet products listed above, utilizes what might otherwise be waste products to make building materials. Hardboard is made of cellulosic (wood) fibers bonded together at high pressures. The material is very dense. It is made in ⅛-inch or ³/₁₆-inch thicknesses, and is used for furniture construction, as the bottom of cabinet drawers, or as the back or wall side of furniture or cabinets. Hardboard is smooth on one face and embossed on the opposite face.

Tempered hardboard is hardboard that is heat-treated to improve its strength and moisture resistance. When drilled in evenly spaced holes of uniform diameter, it may be nailed on the shop wall and used to hang tools, or it may be used for decorative purposes. It is then called pegboard or perforated hardboard. Hardboard may also be made into siding, such as Masonite™. Hardboard siding is usually pre-primed at the factory.

PLYWOOD

To make plywood, logs are sliced or peeled into thin layers or *plies*. Then two or more plies are bonded together with adhesives to make plywood panels. Depending on the quality of the outer wood plies, the plywood may be graded from A through D. For example, oak plywood may be graded "A-A," meaning that both sides or faces of the plywood are high-quality and free of knots or other blemishes. A-A plywood is used for cabinetry or other uses where both sides will be exposed to view—for example, for kitchen cabinet doors. For rough use, where strength is important but appearance is not, the plywood might carry a C-D rating, meaning that one side may have splits or tight knots, the other side may have unrepaired knotholes. C-D grade plywood is the designation for sheathing plywood, used as subfloor or for wall or roof sheathing, where it will be covered with either siding or roofing and appearance is not important. Where one side or surface on plywood is better than the other, for example "A-C," the best or A side is called the *face*.

Plywood also is graded according to its moisture exposure rating. Plywood that is marked "Exterior" is made with waterproof glue, as is "Marine" plywood, which is commonly used for boat construction. "Exposure 1" plywood means the plywood can be used for sheathing, and will later be protected by siding or roofing.

Sheathing grade plywood will also have a span rating, shown on the grade label: 32/16 span rating means that the plywood can be used with a truss span of 32 inches on a roof, but only a 16-inch span is allowed over floor joists. The lower 16-inch span limit for floor use is because the floor will carry a *live load* rating, which means that the floor will have to support the weight of people, furniture, and appliances in addition to supporting the building itself. (The weight of the building itself is called the *dead load*.) See the sample Plywood Markings illustration for a complete review of plywood markings information and its meaning.

The interior or center ply construction of a sheet of plywood can also be important. For example, for some sheathing plywood it is not important that interior or core plies might have large voids or knot holes, as long as strength is not affected. For furniture or cabinet making, hollows or voids in interior plies will show up as rough damaged edges (called "core gap") when the plywood is cut into a table top or made into cabinet drawer fronts or doors. For some furniture applications, the plywood may be designated as "lumbercore," meaning the center ply is made of solid lumber. Lumbercore is a superior choice for making furniture or cabinets.

PANELING

Paneling is a versatile material, usually used to cover walls but also used for its dramatic effect on ceilings. When used on ceilings the 4 x 8 sheets of paneling are installed over wallboard and nailed or glued in place. The panels are installed perpendicular to the joist direction. Then wood beams are installed at 4-foot intervals, or 4 ft. o.c. (on center, or center-to-center). This technique means that the wood beams will cover the end joints of the paneling, so there are no unsightly butt joints to mar the project.

Paneling may be made of solid wood plies, either finished or unfinished, in any one of dozens of colors, wood tones, and wood species. Or paneling may be made of hardboard, with a vinyl photo image of wood grain laminated to the base material. The pre-finished variety, used most often by the do-it-yourselfer, is usually sold in 4' x 8' sheets, in thicknesses of $3/16$ inch to $5/16$ inch. Solid wood paneling such as knotty pine or pecky cypress is often sold in tongue-and-groove planks. The planks are usually $3/4$-inch thick, so no backer board is needed as a base for solid wood paneling. However, you must nail horizontal 2 x 4 nailers between the studs or joists to provide adequate bearing and nailing surfaces.

The thin sheets of pre-finished paneling are not made to be installed directly over stud walls. The panels are too thin, they are noisy, and they will often warp and become wavy between the studs. Instead, a layer of $3/8$-inch thick wallboard must be applied over the studs, then the paneling is glued or glued and nailed over the wallboard. This technique results in a wall that is as thick as plaster ($3/8"$ + $3/8"$ = $3/4"$ thick) and has good stiffness, soundproofing, and resistance to impact damage. This strength plus the ease of cleaning paneling make it a prime choice for game or recreation room walls, for wainscoting in kitchens or dining rooms, and for halls or entry foyers. In addition, the warm wood look enhances the appearance of an office or a study.

Painted nails, with heads colored to match the color or tone of the paneling, can be used for installing paneling. If you use nails, choose nail locations carefully to try to hide them from view. For example, position the nails in the wood grooves of the paneling, or in knots or wood grain where the nail holes will be less visible.

Use a saw guide to ensure a straight cut saw when ripping plywood. Photo courtesy Sears.

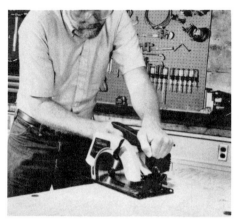

Plywood is easy to work with ordinary hand and power tools. Wear goggles and use a sharp plywood blade for cutting plywood. Photo courtesy Sears.

To avoid splintering the face of paneling, lay the panel face down when using a power saw. This way, the blade will cut through the finish side on the upstroke. Photo courtesy Plywood Paneling Council.

Use panel adhesive to eliminate nail holes in the face of the finish paneling. Tack the panels in position with a few nails at the top of the panel, then use a padded 2 x 4 block and a mallet to tap the panel into full contact with the backer or wall. Paneling lets you "nail the finish on." Photo courtesy Plywood Paneling Council.

Wallboard is an inexpensive choice for walls or ceilings in new construction, or for getting a new surface when applied over existing walls. It is a good do-it-yourself material and is easy to cut and install, using ordinary shop tools. Photo courtesy United States Gypsum.

Wallboard can be nailed in place, but using wallboard screws and a screwgun makes a neater job with fewer fastener failures. Photo courtesy United States Gypsum.

Wallboard can be applied with accessory items such as the resilient metal channel shown. The resilient channel will make the surface more soundproof, and it can be shimmed and used as a means of leveling a ceiling that is not level. You must use self-tapping wallboard screws and a screwgun to install wallboard over steel channel. Photo courtesy Gold Bond Products.

The best way to install paneling is to use a panel adhesive such as Liquid Nails or PL200. Make all the paneling cuts and cutouts and test fit the panel in place to be sure it fits. Then use a caulk gun to apply an S-shaped or serpentine bead over the back side of the panel. Position the panel against the wallboard backer material and hang it in place with a couple of nails driven at the top edge of the panel. Push the panel against the wallboard so that it has full contact with the panel adhesive, then pull the panel away from the wall so air can reach the adhesive. Then push the panel against the wallboard backer and use the side of your fist or a padded 2 x 4 block and hammer to tap on the face of the board and ensure full adhesive contact between the panel and the wallboard backer. If necessary, drive a couple of extra nails along the bottom edge of the panel, where the nailheads will be covered by base trim, to hold it in place until the adhesive cures and provides full panel support.

Buy your paneling at least one week in advance of the installation job, to give the material a chance to acclimate, or to come into temperature and moisture balance with the area where it will be installed. Paneling manufacturers point out that paneling that has been properly handled, transported, and stored should not shrink at the job site. That is true, but we do not know how the material has been handled, and nothing is lost if we follow the old carpenter's rule of letting all materials acclimate before we install them. This is simple insurance against having the materials shrink or swell in place, resulting in panels with shrinkage gaps at the joints, or panels that buckle from expansion.

TIP for buyers: Because paneling is moved about using forklifts, the ends of paneling sometimes get bumped and damaged. This of course greatly reduces the value of the paneling, because it cannot be sold for installation on walls that are a full 8-feet high. Often, however, the do-it-yourselfer may plan a job where the wall to be covered is not a full 8-feet high; for example, in a basement or an attic expansion where ceilings are less than 8-feet high. The tip is to measure the height of the paneling you will need and calculate how many inches must be cut off each panel. Then shop the reject section of the home center for end-damaged paneling. You may get a bargain, because the damaged ends of the panels must be cut off anyway. This way, you may buy a high grade of paneling at distress prices, perhaps for less money than you would pay for the cheapest grades.

The paneling you choose will depend on your own tastes and budget. As in all purchases, keep in mind that a few dollars extra cost per panel should not convince you to buy the cheapest paneling. Remember, you will have to live with your choice a long time and look at it daily. Don't you deserve the best?

WALLBOARD

Wallboard is available in thicknesses of ¼ inch, ³/₈ inch, ½ inch, and ⁵/₈ inch. This thickness range may at first glance seem limiting, because greater wall thickness (mass) is needed to achieve better soundproofing or fireproofing in a wall or ceiling. However, you can apply several layers of wallboard to achieve any wall thickness you want, for whatever purpose. For example, two layers of ³/₈-inch thick wallboard are often laminated together and used to match the ³/₄-inch thickness of older plaster walls. This technique is often used by remodelers to fill in holes or voids in plaster, and to bring the new area into alignment to match the old plaster wall. Also, this wall thickness has better soundproofing and fireproofing qualities. For example, if you are building a duplex, applying two layers of ³/₈-inch thick wallboard on both sides of the common wall (wall between two living units) will help prevent sound transfer between the two units, and will also prevent any fire from traveling through the common wall and consuming both units.

Why offer so many different thicknesses of wallboard? Keep in mind that each time you increase the thickness of a wallboard panel by even $1/8$ inch, that $1/8$ inch is solid plaster, so you gain a great deal of strength and stiffness in the panel with each $1/8$-inch increase in thickness. The following points explain the need and uses for each thickness of wallboard:

¼ inch: Not a stock item at most lumber yards and home centers, ¼-inch wallboard is used as a new skin for old walls. This wallboard can be adhesive-laminated over old plaster to give it a "new skin"— an unbroken new decorating surface. Your supplier will have to special-order ¼-inch wallboard for you.

³/₈ inch: This is also a remodeling grade of wallboard. It is not strong enough to be used as a single layer wall finish, although you may find some post-World War II houses, built before the code standards were changed, that have only ³/₈-inch thick wallboard on walls and/or ceilings. This thickness can be used as a first layer or underlayment base for applying paneling, or can be adhesive-applied in two layers to get a laminated wallboard finish. Laminated wallboard is considered the best of all walls, because it can be built in a short time and provides the soundproofing and fireproofing qualities of the thicker plaster walls, but is virtually crack-proof if it is properly applied. To have a laminated wallboard job, the first layer of wallboard is nailed or screwed to the walls and ceilings, with the base wallboard parallel to the framing joists or studs. The second layer of wallboard is then adhesive-laminated (glued) over the first layer, but the second layer is applied so the panels are perpendicular to the framing. By applying one layer of wallboard parallel to the framing and the second layer perpendicular to the framing, you ensure that the joints are staggered so they do not occur at the same point on the wall or ceiling.

½ inch: Because the thinner ³/₈-inch wallboard sagged between studs or joists, ½-inch thick wallboard quickly became the standard of the industry in postwar housing. This wallboard can be used in single-layer applications for a finished wall or ceiling. Caution: Because of the fact that roof trusses are now set 24 inches on center (o.c.) rather than 16 inches o.c. as were the ceiling joists in stick framing, and because heavier thicknesses of insulation are now installed on top of wallboard ceilings, ⁵/₈-inch thick wallboard is now advised for these ceiling applications, to eliminate wallboard sagging between ceiling joists. The wider spacing and the heavier insulation loads must have a stiffer wallboard panel to avoid sagging.

⁵/₈ inch: Wallboard starts to get pretty heavy when it is ⁵/₈-inch thick, so this is the thickest wallboard you can buy. For greater thicknesses you must apply multiple layers of wallboard. As mentioned above, you should apply ⁵/₈-inch thick wallboard on ceilings where joist or truss spacing is 24 inches o.c. or greater. This wallboard is also specified for firewalls. The wallboard commonly referred to as "⁵/₈" Firecode" must be used on the common wall between a house and an attached garage, and on the garage ceiling. The reason for this requirement is that ½-inch thick wallboard has a fire rating of 45 minutes, which means that if burning house temperatures are applied to one side of a wall with ½-inch wallboard, the framing inside the wall will start to char or combust after 45 minutes. Wallboard designated ⁵/₈" Firecode has a full 60-minute fire rating, which means that framing covered with the ⁵/₈" Firecode will combust after 60 minutes. This means that the homeowner gains 15 precious minutes in which to detect and report any fire.

In addition to a variety of thicknesses, wallboard is

made in different lengths for special applications. The most common length in home centers is 8 feet, although using 12-foot long wallboard will give you a much better job, with fewer seams to finish and with greater wall strength. Although many texts show wallboard being applied parallel to the framing, i.e., 8-foot long panels "stood up" on the walls, all manufacturers and the Gypsum Association recommend that the best job is obtained when you install 12-foot long panels perpendicular to the framing. This results in fewer joints to treat, a stronger wall (ties together the maximum number of studs or joists), and joints that are easier to hide. "Joint banding," a defect in which paint over joints appears to be darker or "shadowed," is emphasized when wallboard is applied parallel to the framing. Another argument: standing wallboard up, or installing it parallel to the studs, invariably will result in having joints above or at the top corners of doors or windows. This results in cracks, and in joints treated at the corners where you will have difficulty in trying to fit mitered trim. Use the longest wallboard panels you can handle and apply them perpendicular to the framing. If this seems too difficult, it is much better to hire professionals to install the wallboard properly than to do it yourself and end up with inferior results from applying the wallboard parallel to the framing.

Tips to Remember when Installing Wallboard

* Use wallboard adhesives where possible, augmented by wallboard screws positioned as directed by the adhesive manufacturer. Wallboard nails are the very worst choice for installing wallboard, because the repeated blows of the hammer often damage the face of the wallboard panel, and nails are more prone to "pop." Do not use nails.

* Where there is a vapor barrier that prevents using wallboard adhesives, such as on exterior walls and on the ceiling next to the attic, use a screw gun to drive wallboard screws. Screw length is important to prevent pops: use only 1-inch screws to install ½-inch wallboard, and 1¼-inch screws to install ⅝-inch thick wallboard. Nails or screws that are too long cause pops or "fastener failures," because the fasteners pop when the wood framing shrinks.

* Inspect wallboard panels before you buy them and after delivery. Wallboard panels often are cracked, or the corners of the panels damaged, during delivery. Do not accept or try to finish or repair damaged wallboard. It is difficult enough to get a good job finishing wallboard when the panels are not damaged: don't make the job more difficult by trying to finish cracked or damaged panels.

CEMENT BOARD (DUROCK)

Once upon a time all ceramic tile was set on a base of solid concrete. Walls to be tiled were covered with wire lath, then plastered with a full 1-inch layer of concrete. Then came tile adhesives and wallboard construction, and we tried to glue the tile directly to wallboard. The trouble was, we neglected maintaining the grout between the tile, and water penetrated between the tile joints and destroyed the wallboard base, which of course meant that the tile fell on the floor. End of expensive tile job. Enter cement board, known by its trade name of Durock™. Cement board is made of cement and fiberglass fibers and is used as an underlayment for ceramic tile. Cement board will not wick up water and does not fall apart when it is wet. It is easy to cut and nail, and is the best substrate for use in tub or shower areas where you will have ceramic tile. It can also be used for floors or as a ceramic tile base on cabinet countertops. An exterior cement board can be used as a base for applying stucco.

6.
Glues and Adhesives

Not many years ago all available glues were animal glues, made from blood, hides, hooves, milk (casein), or other animal products. Modern glue and adhesive technology has produced hot melt glues, epoxy glues, combination adhesive/caulks, and all-purpose adhesives. All these products are vastly superior to the products available only a generation ago. But choosing a product for a particular glue or adhesive application may be more difficult than ever, given the array of products the consumer will encounter on a shopping trip. We will try to present a basic review of the most common types of glues and adhesives. But first, some helpful advice.

TIPS FOR USING GLUES AND ADHESIVES SUCCESSFULLY

- The surfaces to be glued together must be smooth and free of dirt or grease.

- Observe label instructions carefully. Take proper note of temperature and moisture requirements for using your product.

- Sand or plane board edges to be sure they match and fit together without gaps. Most glues are not intended to fill any gaps be-

tween workpieces. Invest in a joiner/planer if you are building furniture or cabinetry, to ensure that you can make a proper, tight-fitting wood joint.

- More glue is not better. The warning of the glue industry is "the thinner the glue line, the better the bond." Apply glue sparingly to glue surfaces and follow label directions.

- All-purpose household glues work well for most of your repair needs. For repairing expensive items such as fine china or furniture, ask your dealer to suggest a glue made specifically for your purpose, or consider having the repair professionally done.

- Handle all glues and adhesives with care. Use them with plenty of ventilation, and avoid skin or eye contact with the materials.

Here is a quick look at glues and adhesives that will do almost any job you have at hand.

HOUSEHOLD GLUES

An all-purpose adhesive will work for most house

repairs. One such product we've used with success is ELMER'S STIX-ALL, an adhesive product distributed by Borden Inc. Label information includes the fact that cure time of the adhesive depends on a variety of factors, including porosity of the material glued and the temperature and humidity in the workplace. If your repair piece will be subjected to water (dishes) or to severe stress (joints in furniture, etc.), seek out an adhesive made especially for that particular type of repair, or pay to have it professionally done.

Industry sources report that, as is the case with many products, most adhesive failures are the result of improper application. Observe label instructions. For example, STIX-ALL can be used after curing for twenty-four hours, but it does not reach maximum strength for three days. Using a product before the glue or adhesive has fully cured can obviously cause a bond failure. Also, it is important to remove old glue residue from furniture legs or braces before regluing them. You may be advised to clamp or tape large or flexible materials together, to hold them immobile until the glue or adhesive cures. Again, follow product label directions.

When doing most glue projects, any excess should be cleaned up quickly before the glue sets. For some jobs, such as gluing new wood, wiping up excess glue may spread the glue over the workpiece and seal the wood pores so the wood will not take stain evenly. For these wood workshop projects, it may be better to let the glue dry, then trim the excess away with a razor blade or sharp chisel. This action will avoid smearing the glue over a wide area.

HOME/SHOP

Hot melt glues, along with the all-purpose glues, have proven to be a favorite consumer product. Because the hot melt glues come in solid form, in glue sticks, there is no messy mixing; the glues set fast, usually within one minute, so they do not need

clamping; cure time is almost instantaneous, so there are no hours-long delays before you can continue to work on, or to use, the workpiece. Glue gun applicators let you place the glue precisely, with less mess, and hot glue can be used for joining wood, paper, tile, and cloth. The hot glue gun is a must for the hobbyist or woodworker.

White glue, sometimes called "carpenter's glue," is another popular household favorite. One familiar white glue product is ELMER'S GLUE-ALL. White glue can be used for gluing wood, paper, cloth, pottery—almost any porous or semi-porous material. Use white glue for shop work and for projects such as gluing wood joints in trim or cabinetry. White glue is slow-setting, so you must use various types of clamps to hold the glue joints immobile when using the glue for furniture or cabinet projects. Check the glue label for suggested clamp time. The clamps can usually be removed after the glue has set overnight. White glue is intended for interior use and should not be used for outdoor projects or for any project that will have water contact.

Yellow (aliphatic) glues are also called "carpenter's glues" and are used for outdoor projects or for any job where exposure to water or moisture is expected. Aliphatic or yellow glues, like white glues, are slow-drying, so you must clamp the workpieces together until full setting has been achieved. Follow label directions carefully.

Epoxy glues may be used where exceptional bonding strength is required. Epoxy glues are two-part glues that require mixing at the time of use, and *pot or open time* (time until they set) is limited. Mix only as much as you will use within the label time limits, and observe the recommended ratio between resin and hardener. Epoxy glues may be the most difficult for the consumer to use, and you should seek simpler alternatives to epoxies when possible.

Adhesive caulks such as Polyseamseal™ All-Purpose Adhesive Caulk can be used both as an adhesive and as a crack-sealing caulk. Use to fill wall and floor cracks and to seal joints around bathtubs or showers, gutters, windows, and boat portholes. The products can also be used to glue and embed loose ceramic tile, paneling, glass, and countertops.

CONSTRUCTION ADHESIVES

A boon to pro and amateur alike has been the development of a variety of construction adhesives. These adhesives are available in either quart- or gallon-size pails or in caulk tubes for accurate, no-mess application. Obvious candidates for adhesive application include joining any materials that cannot easily be joined with nails or screws, such as joining wood or other building materials to concrete walls or floors or to steel beams. But adhesives are recommended for producing more professional-looking results and for making any job easier, even those jobs that could be done using metal fasteners (screws or nails).

Often, the homeowner will elect not to use construction adhesives, thinking that the adhesives are an expensive and unnecessary "extra." But consider the advantages of using construction adhesives before you decide to settle for using nails only.

One plus for adhesives is that they reduce the need for metal fasteners. Often, using an adhesive means reducing the number of nails or screws needed by 50 percent, or even more. Fewer fasteners means fewer fastener failures, such as split wood, nail pops, nail rusting and rust or corrosion stains, and damage from hammer blows that miss the nail and damage the workpiece. Adhesives will also help bridge gaps from misaligned framing. Using a construction adhesive to secure floor sheathing plywood to floor joists can mean a stronger, more squeak-free floor. The same technique can be used for building decks, and can eliminate popped nails

in deck boards that can puncture bare feet.

PANELING ADHESIVES

Use caulk-tube adhesives designated for general purpose interior or paneling applications, such as PL200 or Liquid Nails, when installing wood paneling. The adhesives can be applied with a caulk gun, in an "S" pattern on the backside of the panels. For instructions on installing paneling, see the appropriate section in Chapter 5. One way to ensure full contact with the adhesive is to wrap a scrap 2 x 4 block with duct tape (to pad the block so it won't damage the paneling), lay the block against the panel, and tap the 2 x 4 block with a hammer or mallet, moving the block over the entire surface of the panel as you repeatedly tap it. Using a panel adhesive eliminates nails, so there are no nail holes or nail heads to worry about; it prevents damage to the panel due to blows from hammer heads that miss the nails; and it bridges over slight misalignments in the framing, which results in a straighter, flatter wall. By all means, explore the various kinds of construction adhesives available before you start your building or remodeling project.

DECK AND FLOOR ADHESIVE

Using a deck and floor adhesive can make a stronger, squeak-free deck or floor. There are no nails to loosen and squeak when the floor is flexed as you walk. Using a caulk gun, adhesives are applied in 3/8-inch beads across the upper edge of the floor or deck joist. Then the deck board or 1/2-inch plywood sheathing is placed on the joists. Some adhesives may call for perimeter nailing of the 4' x 8' plywood sheets, or for a few temporary nails in deck boards, to hold the material in place until the adhesive sets. Not only does the adhesive eliminate squeaks and make a stronger deck, there are no nails or screws to pop up and snag clothing or puncture bare feet or skin. One good deck adhesive, warranted for exterior use, is PL500 Deck and Dock Adhesive. This adhesive product is warranted even for use on boat docks or diving platforms that are constantly exposed to moisture and water.

WALLBOARD ADHESIVES

Wallboard adhesives address many of the problems we've talked about generally, but because nail or screw pops on wallboard cause objectionable blemishes on the interior wall or ceiling, we especially recommend adhesives for wallboard construction. There are areas where adhesives cannot be used, and you should use wallboard screws, not nails, for securing wallboard in these areas. The areas where adhesives cannot be used include exterior walls, where the kraft paper or polyethylene plastic vapor barrier prohibits the use of adhesives. Ceiling wallboard also cannot be fastened with adhesives where there is a vapor barrier (usually only in the ceiling between the top floor of the house and the attic space, not between floors). Again, for installing wallboard on these ceilings where you cannot use adhesives, use wallboard screws alone, not wallboard nails.

Wallboard adhesives also are very useful for installing wallboard over pre-framed pocket doors or on soffits, where the nailers may be 1 x 4 lumber. Because the thin lumber flexes as it is nailed, it is almost impossible to drive wallboard nails into 1 x 4s. One-inch long wallboard screws can, of course, be driven using an electric screw gun, without the impact problems that are common with driving nails. But in areas such as for fastening wallboard to pocket door frames, where future vibration may occur if the door is slammed, wallboard adhesive offers a superior, "pop-free" installation method.

POTPOURRI

There are, of course, other uses for construction adhesives. Most any of the caulk-tube construction adhesive products can be used to attach furring strips or studs to concrete or concrete block walls, or to fasten the bottom 2 x 4 plate to the concrete floor. Adhesives can also be used to fasten 2 x 4s or other framing to steel beams or posts—finishing off a basement is one example.

You can also use any all-purpose construction adhesive to secure laminated countertops to kitchen cabinets or to bathroom vanity cabinets, or for almost any fastening job. Keep in mind that it will be very difficult to dismantle any project that you build using adhesives. One last tip would be to check the product to see if it is intended for interior or exterior applications, to be sure it is intended for use on your particular project.

Contact adhesives are so called because they have no set time: i.e., they set on contact. Contact adhesives are most commonly used for laminating decorative plastic laminates such as Formica to plywood countertops or furniture. Time was when contact adhesives were very potent chemicals, with highly volatile bases. These contact adhesives are now forbidden, and today's products are water based. There is no danger from working with contact adhesives, keeping in mind that you should always read and heed label instructions for working with any chemical substance.

TIP: You can't move or adjust materials, once they have come into contact, when you are using contact adhesives. Assemble a bundle of wood lath, or old slats from venetian blinds, when you are working with contact adhesive. Position the lath or blind slats on the surface after the contact adhesive has tacked or become dry to the touch. Position the plastic laminate or other material carefully over the base, then pull the lath or blind slats out, one by one, while carefully matching the laminate to the substrate or base material. This procedure will ensure that you do not inadvertently let the laminate come in contact with the substrate before the laminate is properly aligned.

There are also adhesives, packaged in bulk in quart, gallon, or multi-gallon pails, that are made for trowel application. These bulk adhesives are usually spread with a notched spreader or trowel, and are used to install floor tile or other flooring, sheet vinyl, ceramic tile, or even for installing carpet. For these bulk adhesives, used for specific material installation, it is best to buy the adhesive where you buy the other material: i.e., buy ceramic tile adhesive when you buy the ceramic tile, and buy vinyl floor covering adhesive at the floor covering store. Trying to select tile or other adhesive on the basis of price alone, from among the variety of adhesives offered at home centers, may result in your choosing the wrong adhesive for your particular project or application. The plus for this plan is that the dealer who sells you the tile, vinyl, or whatever material must provide a warranty for the entire materials package, which is an obvious advantage should you have problems with the job.

7.
Primers and Sealers

Many building materials have surfaces with uneven porosity that will not take paint well without a preparatory coating. A single wood board, for example, may have both hard and soft fiber layers; may have knots and open grain; and may have both open and closed grain in the same board. If you attempt to paint that board without priming it, the paint will be absorbed unequally into the wood, may lie unevenly on the surface, and may therefore have a mottled or varying sheen or gloss.

For this reason most surfaces to be painted should have a first coating of primer, a specially formulated material that is applied directly over the bare wood (or other) surface. Primers contain pigments and fillers that help to even out any differences in surface texture and to present a uniform surface for applying the finish coat. Primers make the paint surface uniform and also provide a proper base to which the paint can adhere.

Sealers are formulated with a high resin content to create a film or barrier so that water or paint solvent cannot penetrate the surface. Sealers equalize the porosity or suction of the surface to be painted, so that the finish coat will lie evenly as a protective coating on the surface of the workpiece and will not soak into the material. This ensures a better appearance, because painting a surface with uneven suction or porosity may cause both the color and the gloss level or sheen of the finish coat to appear uneven or patchy.

PRIMING—EXTERIOR

Many new wood siding products, including hardboard siding such as Masonite, come pre-primed from the manufacturer. Some are even back-primed to prevent moisture from entering into the siding from the back or unfinished side, causing paint peeling or failure on the exterior or exposed face of the siding. Apply a prime coat and two coats of paint to most unpainted wood siding.

Most manufacturing representatives, such as the The California Redwood Association (CRA), recommend back-priming new siding before you install it. But advice for what kind of primer to use can vary. California Redwood Association, for example, recommends that you use a stain-blocking

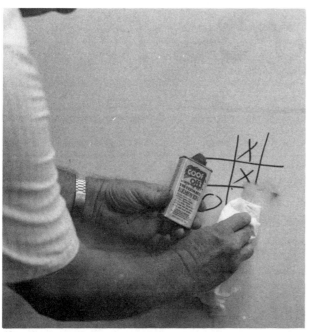

If walls or ceilings are stained, first use a stain remover to take off as much of the stain material as possible. Use a clean cloth, soaked in the stain remover, to wipe the stain away. Author photo.

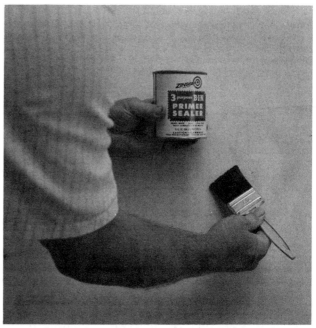

Use a shellac-base sealer such as BIN to cover any difficult stain, from smoke to crayons. Author photo.

Sheetrock® First Coat is a latex primer formulated especially for first coat application on new wallboard. Photo courtesy United States Gypsum.

Do not use any paint as an "all-purpose" finish. Choose paints formulated especially for your application. For example, use a masonry waterproofer paint for concrete basement walls. Photo courtesy UGL.

This shot of a peeling gutter illustrates the results of using unthinned house paint to paint metal rain gutters. The heavy paint film will crack and peel as the metal gutters expand and contract with temperature changes. Rather, choose a metal paint product for painting gutters.

Clean chalked paint off aluminum siding using a wood-cleaning product such as DEKSWOOD. Then repaint the aluminum siding with a quality acrylic latex house paint.

Use a wood deck cleaner and a stiff scrub brush to clean any exterior wood structure, such as this timber retaining wall. Author photo.

latex primer for a prime coat on their air-seasoned or unseasoned siding; for kiln-dried siding they recommend using an oil or alkyd resin base primer, no matter the choice of the topcoat. But, regardless of which primer you use, they recommend using a latex product as the top or finish coat of paint. Sound confusing? It needn't be: just ask the siding supplier or a trusted paint dealer (one who sells to professional painters) to help you select the right primer and finish paint for your project. (Also, see the paint/stain charts in Chapter 8.) When finishing new wood with stains or bleaching oils just apply two coats of the stain, or follow the directions given by the manufacturer.

When choosing remodeling materials, consider immediate and future finishing requirements. New windows, for example, are available with vinyl or pre-finished aluminum cladding, so they will not need paint or stain for many years. The same is true of soffits, trim boards, and siding. Remember that pre-painted products have the finish applied in a factory, under optimum conditions, with temperature and moisture levels under strict control. These conditions (plus the manufacturers' warranties) ensure against premature failure of the paint or stain finish. Pre-finished materials let you "nail the paint on" as you install the product, so you avoid the mess, waste, and poor conditions that may adversely effect a painting job completed at the building/construction site.

When repainting a house over old paint, you may use the old paint coat as a primer coat, assuming the paint is intact and not peeled. Then just clean (power wash) the old paint surface and sand lightly as required. If you must remove peeled paint over small surfaces, spot prime the repair areas. If the old paint is removed completely, or over a wide area, it is best to prime the entire building, or one side of the house if peeling is limited to only one side.

PRIMING—INTERIOR

When redecorating an older house that has no vapor barrier in the exterior walls and/or ceilings, you can establish a vapor barrier by applying a coat of oil-base primer over the surfaces in question. This oil-base primer provides a suitable film to reduce moisture transmission through the wall or ceiling. Be sure to remove any electrical outlet covers and heating duct registers before priming to ensure complete coverage. If there are cracks between the outlets and the plaster or wallboard, fill the cracks with spackle before priming the wall to make the vapor barrier as complete as possible.

In most cases any sound, existing paint finish will serve as a base or "primer" for repainting walls or ceilings. If these surfaces have been widely repaired, apply a coat of primer over the entire wall or ceiling before painting. Spot priming is possible for small repair areas, but keep in mind that these well-primed spots may look "shiny" when repainted and compared to the unprimed areas of the wall or ceiling. If you plan to apply wall covering to the surface (wall or ceiling), applying an alkyd primer over the entire area is recommended, to provide a tight seal and to ensure easy removal of the wall covering in the future.

Priming Textured Ceilings

Along about the mid-'50s the ceiling finish of choice became some sort of texture, either hand or machine (spray) applied. Most of these texture materials were extremely soft and provided no seal for easy cleaning or for repainting. As a result these unprimed ceilings are almost impossible to repaint, because their soft, absorbent surface will take paint unevenly. Lap or roller marks plus uneven paint film result if you apply any ceiling paint over an unprimed texture paint surface. To prevent this uneven application you must apply a coat of alkyd primer over the texture, then finish with the top coat of choice. We suggest that you buy a quality latex paint and roll it over the primed texture ceiling. Choose a latex paint designated "Ceiling Flat White," or one with a very flat sheen. Any gloss on the finish coat will highlight ceiling defects: the flatter the better, when it comes to the gloss of any paint, and it is especially important for ceilings. Ceilings are the largest unbroken surfaces in a house — unbroken by openings such as windows and doors, or by furniture placement—so you must choose a ceiling paint that has very low gloss, and thus very little light reflection, to have a flattering ceiling finish.

Priming for Smoke, Difficult Stains

Smoke stains from either tobacco or from a house fire are very difficult to cover. Nicotine in the tobacco smoke and grease or oil in the house fire smoke will bleed through latex paints, because the water in latex paints will activate the staining agent. The same thing is true of rust stains that damage plaster or wallboard from leaking radiators or hot water pipes. In most cases you can clean smoke from the wall or ceiling surface using a cleaner such as TSP (trisodium phosphate). Remove as much of the smoke as possible. For limited smoke damage, apply a coat of alkyd primer over the affected surface. For very difficult stains a fast-drying shellac sealer such as BIN will be a better choice. BIN will seal over smoke, oil, rust, crayon, or markers. If you use a shellac-base sealer such as BIN you must use alcohol as a solvent to clean up spills, spatters, and tools.

Priming New Wallboard

Wallboard presents a perfect example of why we need primers and sealers. Newly finished wallboard offers two distinctly different surfaces to be decorated: the face paper of the wallboard over the field or untreated area of the wallboard, and the taping compound over the seams, corners, and screws or nails. Paint applied to the face paper and the compound will be absorbed unequally and will exhibit problems such as "joint banding," a phenomenon that makes the paint appear shadowed, or darker, over the areas treated with compound.

Some texts recommend using oil-base primers over wallboard, but the Gypsum Association and its member firms have never recommended this practice. Oil-base primers are slow drying, and tend to soak into and raise the nap on the face paper of the wallboard. But the oil-base primer will dry smooth over areas that are treated with taping compound. The result is a mess, with a blotchy surface that is alternately rough and smooth. The only (new) wallboard surface that should be primed with oil-base or alkyd primer is any surface that will be finished with a texture paint, such as ceilings that will be spray-textured. For any other surface, the wallboard industry advises using a heavy-bodied latex paint as a first or prime coat.

For years the paint industry offered "primer-sealers" for first-coat application on wallboard, but there are distinct differences between primers and sealers. The problem is that many primers do not contain the proper type and amount of pigments and fillers to conceal the surface texture differences on wallboard.

By the same token, sealers may have a high resin content to provide a film that prevents penetration of water or paint solvent, thereby equalizing the porosity of the wallboard surfaces, but this film cannot eliminate the surface texture differences of the wallboard. Neither primers nor sealers are recommended as a first coat on gypsum wallboard. Use an undiluted interior flat latex wall paint for the first or prime coat on wallboard. When this first coat is dry, you can apply a finish coat of any sheen or gloss paint finish.

Our favorite choice as a first coat on wallboard is a

latex primer named, oddly enough, Sheetrock® First Coat. A product of the United States Gypsum Co., First Coat is available either in powder form, to be mixed with water, or factory mixed in paint form. The product is fast-drying for quicker re-coating, seals the surface to equalize paint absorption, and minimizes surface texture variations. Ask your dealer to order First Coat for you if you don't see it in stock.

Note that United States Gypsum (USG), the inventor of Sheetrock and a major manufacturer of wallboard and wallboard products, does not suggest oil-base primers as a first or primer coat on walls or ceilings that will be decorated with wall coverings. Rather, USG advises that a prime application of First Coat should be followed with a coat of sizing prior to hanging wall covering.

Clear Wood Sealers

The time-honored method of finishing woodwork or furniture, to have a natural wood finish, was to apply a clear sealer, then apply a polyurethane or varnish finish as a topcoat. Or a stain was applied to give the wood a preferred tone or color. The stain was followed by sealer (sometimes called a "sanding sealer") to minimize the absorption across the surface of the wood. The sealer would raise the grain of the wood, so sanding was necessary before the finish coat of varnish or other finish was applied. Today, some wood finishes may combine sealer and finish, or even include the stain, so that a wipe-on product provides acceptable results with a minimum of effort and skill. However, any finish product will tend to raise the grain of the wood, so you should sand between coats using a fine sandpaper. This sanding between coats will also remove any airborne lint or dust that has settled on the wet finish, and ensure that your finished project is smooth and blemish-free.

CONCLUSION

Basic painting wisdom tells us that any surface to be repainted should be clean, dry, and free from peeling or excessive chalking. Beyond these basic and rather obvious criteria, when should you use a primer or a sealer? For best results, you should always use a primer as a first coat on new materials. Also, apply a primer on any surface that has been extensively repaired, such as a cracked plaster wall or ceiling, to equalize the suction between the new repair areas and the old plaster. If the old exterior paint is peeling, or extensive sanding has been necessary, apply a primer over the entire surface. If a house interior has been damaged by smoke or fire, first clean the smoke residue away, using trisodium phosphate (TSP) or an equally strong cleaner. Then prime the smoke-damaged areas to seal in the smoke and prevent it from being activated and bleeding through the new paint finish. For sealing over difficult stains such as smoke, grease, or oil, a shellac sealer is recommended.

If the budget is a concern but you feel the surface needs priming, you can have the paint dealer tint the primer slightly to match the color of the finish paint coat, so you can get by with a two-coat job. For priming on wallboard interiors, pro painters often consider a heavy-bodied paint as being "self-priming," so the finish coat is limited to two coats of latex paint. The basic rule is always to follow the paint manufacturers' label instructions when painting, and when in doubt, use a primer or sealer.

8.
Paints and Stains

Some years ago, while working on a book about painting, I interviewed a fellow who had thirty years of experience in the retail paint industry. I knew of his frustration with consumer complaints, and that most of those consumer paint problems were the result of do-it-yourself mistakes. My question to him was: "If you could give advice to perhaps thousands of readers, what would that advice be?" With little hesitation he replied: "Tell them to read the label on the paint can. Paint dealers see the returned paint, and hear all the complaints. Most paint problems occur because people fail to read and heed the advice we give to them. Part of this is a general feeling that "anyone can paint." But people also assume that one paint is like another, and use the wrong paint for the surface they're painting. Or they mix in leftover paint they have at home, in order to save it, and the two paints are not compatible. When the job fails they always blame the product. Paint chemistry is advanced and we do a lot of research. Paint quality rarely is the problem."

READ THE LABEL

Advice to read the label may seem elementary. Yet because painting is the most commonly-done do-it-yourself activity, many of us believe that painting is a simple chore, when in fact one must follow professional procedure to get a good paint job. Those who believe "anyone can paint" should check out the number of defective paint jobs in their own neighborhood.

Following is a list of things you can learn simply by reading the label on the paint can. Check the label at the paint store to get such basic information as the manufacturer, the warranty, and the suitability of the product for your particular project. When you get the paint home and before starting to paint, sit down with a cup of coffee and read all the application information. That will be the most rewarding ten minutes of the entire project, and will ensure the ultimate success of the paint job.

MANUFACTURER AND WARRANTY

A number of the home-oriented magazines, such as *Consumer Reports*, do periodic tests of various types and brands of paints and stains. To buy a top paint product, check out these test results and

Protect exterior wood surfaces such as these porch steps with DAP Woodlife. Photo courtesy USG.

Use a paint sponge to apply deck finish to the cracks between deck boards. Cuprinol Deck Stain & Preservative shown should be applied every second year to ensure wood protection. Photo courtesy Darworth Inc.

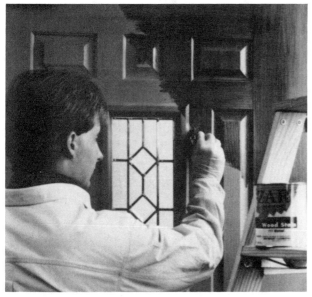

ZAR Wood Stain (and sealer) is a superior but low-cost finish product for use on fiberglass, steel, or wood doors. Photo courtesy UGL.

UGL also makes a wood-graining tool for tooling a grain pattern on a fiberglass, steel, or wood door. Photo courtesy UGL.

choose a paint that is made by a major manufacturer. The major players in the business have invested millions to ensure that paint is formulated to perform as warranted.

Check also the label warranty information. Exterior paints today are warranted to last for ten to fifteen years. Note that most warranties are limited, meaning the manufacturer limits his own liability to replacing the paint. Because the cost of the paint is a minor point, compared to the labor required to apply the paint, you should buy only the best paint available.

COST

As with all purchasing decisions, you should remember Branson's Second Law, which is: *You don't always get what you pay for, but you never get more than you pay for.* (Branson's First Law is: Murphy was an optimist.) Some products cost more because they are heavily advertised, but most often the price reflects the better-quality ingredients included in the product. For example, the price and grade of pigments such as titanium vary widely in cost, so a paint that is claimed to be "non-yellowing" may have a high grade titanium that will not turn yellow with age, and so will cost more.

I recently checked the price labels on two different latex paints. One paint contained 65 percent water and cost $9 per gallon. The other, claimed to be "our finest interior latex" contained 51 percent water and cost $12 per gallon. Both were interior grade latex paints, and both were on sale. Which was the cheaper? The price difference was only $3 per gallon, and the paint with the lower water content—but higher price—no doubt would cover the old paint better and would present a more durable finish for cleaning. Like the auto filter company says, "you can pay me now or pay me later."

RECOMMENDED APPLICATION

Check the label to be sure the paint is recommended for use on your project. Some interior latex paints promise suitability for any interior surface, whether it be wallboard, plaster, wood paneling, or masonry. But I always choose a latex that is labeled "Ceiling Flat White" for ceilings, because the flat sheen will look better and hide defects better on the large, unbroken ceiling surface than an ordinary latex would. For exterior applications that will be exposed to weather I prefer to buy paint that is specifically formulated for the surface I will be painting, not an all-purpose paint. For painting exterior concrete walls, for example, I would buy a masonry paint, not ordinary house paint.

PREPARATION

The amount of surface preparation needed will depend on the brand of paint you choose, plus the surface to which you will apply the product. For example, for painting bare wallboard, some labels advise that you simply apply two coats of their latex paint, on the premise that latex wall paints are "self-sealing." United States Gypsum (USG), a major wallboard manufacturer, recommends a first coat either of a high-solids latex or their First Coat latex primer as a first coat for wallboard. Some paint manufacturers advise using a first coat of either their own particular primer or an enamel undercoater on wallboard. For reasons explained in Chapter 7, Primers and Sealers, we prefer USG First Coat latex on wallboard. We advise never to use an oil-base primer on wallboard. I know that some texts do advise oil primer as a wallboard first coat: the authors of those texts should read the Gypsum Association handbook.

As a further example of the need to read your product label, consider the advice of the California Redwood Association. They advise (see charts) using an alkyd resin primer on new redwood siding,

To prevent paint messes, use a plastic drip tray under the paint pail. Choose a paint brush that matches the job at hand, with your own physical strength in mind. Author photo.

To avoid wasting paint, be sure the paint can is tightly sealed after using. Cover the paint can lid with your paint rag to prevent paint from spattering when lid is replaced. Author photo.

but they also advise using a stain-blocking latex primer if the redwood is air-seasoned or unseasoned. They advise using an exterior latex topcoat, over either the alkyd or the latex primer. Read the label instructions for best results.

SPREAD RATE

Most manufacturers recommend a spread rate of 350-400 square feet per gallon. The spread rate is the number of square feet a gallon of paint should cover, when applied on a pre-painted, smooth surface. New, unpainted surfaces or rough surfaces will obviously soak up more paint and provide less area coverage. The amateur may try to "stretch" the paint, or get more coverage from the gallon. But paint that is applied too thin will not provide good hide or coverage, and the new paint film will be too thin to wash or clean successfully. Mentally check off an area of about 100 square feet, and check to see if you covered that area with one quart of paint. Try to apply the paint at the recommended spread rate. This is especially important when applying any "one coat" paint: obviously you must apply a generous coat if you expect the paint to cover in one coat, as advertised.

TEMPERATURE/HUMIDITY

If you plan to use an oil-base or alkyd paint, you must observe the precautions regarding humidity. For example, you should not apply oil paint over dew-wet siding. If you are using latex paints (and you should, whenever possible), it is less important to watch humidity levels, although conditions that are too dry can cause edge drying and lap marks on any paint. But it is always important to apply paint when temperatures are within the label guidelines, usually between 55 degrees and 80 degrees. Applying paint when temperatures are too hot or too cold can affect the drying time of the paint, and will

result in edge-drying, poor tool function, and an uneven paint job.

DRY/CURE TIME

There are two time frames to observe on the paint label. One is the time required for the paint to dry sufficiently to recoat over it, and the second time limit is the amount of time needed for the paint to reach maximum film toughness for cleaning or scrubbing. It is important to note both these time limits. For example, you should remove any masking tape quickly, as soon as the paint is dry to the touch or too dry to run. This way, if any paint has run under the edge of the masking tape, it is still soft enough to clean up easily. Paint that has reached maximum hardness will be difficult to remove. Fully hardened paint will also make the masking tape hard to remove. So do any cleanup as soon as the paint is dry to the touch.

Don't try to scrub paint until it has fully cured. When paint is dirty, apply the cleaner (soap or detergent and water) in a blotting manner, just wetting the dirt. Do not scrub: you may scratch or remove the paint. Let the dirt soak to loosen and lift it from the paint, then wipe the dirt away gently.

SHEEN/GLOSS

The sheen or gloss level of the paint is an indication of its ability to reflect light. Manufacturers may identify the various gloss levels as "flat" (least sheen), "eggshell," "semi-gloss," and "gloss" (most sheen). Keep in mind that the more sheen or gloss the paint shows, the more it will emphasize any defects in the painted surface. A good rule to follow is the flatter the finish, the better the hide or concealability of the paint. The lesson is that any surface to which you will apply a high gloss finish should receive extra preparation; i.e., apply patchers to

When applying texture paints, use a long-nap paint roller to establish a light-to-heavy stipple pattern. Roughness of the texture depends on the consistency of the paint and the type of applicator used. Photo courtesy USG.

Many paint applicators are made for painting wrought iron, but none does a quicker or more thorough job than the aerosol paint can. Mask or cover any nearby surface that you don't want to paint. Author photo.

The multi-level and rough surfaces of this cedar fence make spray painting a necessity. Cup spray gun can be used for small jobs; rent an airless sprayer for larger projects. Author photo.

smooth any defects and sand the surface thoroughly. Also, you should always apply an alkyd-base primer or enamel undercoater to the surface before applying a high gloss paint. Any unprimed surface will absorb paint unevenly, and this will cause a variation in sheen of the paint finish coat.

The downside or opposite argument is that generally flat finishes do not have as tight a surface seal and therefore are not as easy to clean as glossy finishes are. The more porous flat paint finish will permit dirt or oil to penetrate into the paint film, whereas the gloss paint will keep the dirt on the surface where it can be easily wiped away. The rule is to use flat paints for best "hide" on problem surfaces, such as wavy plaster, and on all ceilings. Most people prefer the look of flat paint in formal rooms, and use gloss paints where there will be human contact (fingerprints), high humidity, or activities such as bathing or cooking.

PAINTING PROBLEM SURFACES

For years, as a home magazine editor and a radio talk-show guest, I have been asked for advice on how to paint problem surfaces. Most exterior paint texts provide advice on how to prepare and paint ordinary wood siding. The problem is, we don't all have wood siding, and advice for painting stucco, aluminum, redwood, or badly chalked exterior paint surfaces may vary from accepted wisdom for painting wood siding. Following is a list of paint tips for painting your extraordinary house.

Chalked Paint

For years the advice for painting chalked surfaces was always to use an alkyd or oil-base paint. That advice has become outdated as new latex paint formulations have been developed. Several latex paints, including Benjamin Moore and Olympic Overcoat, do especially well on chalked surfaces.

The point is, however, that you should not paint over chalked surfaces until you have taken steps to reduce or eliminate the chalking problem.

Chalked paint particles are microscopic in size, and are therefore very difficult to wash away. But several of the exterior wood/deck cleaners offered today are effective when used to clean away chalked paint. One such product that we've personally used is DEKSWOOD, a product of the Flood Company (800-321-3444 in Hudson, OH). DEKSWOOD is a concentrated cleaner that can be used to clean chalked paint from any siding surface. Use the cleaner according to label directions, then wash or power wash it away to clean the surface. Let it dry, then brush on the finish paint. The brush is the best tool for painting chalked surfaces, because the bristle action tends to ensure good paint contact with the surface.

The Flood Company also makes a pre-coat primer for chalking surfaces, called Emulsa-Bond. The product can be used to lock down any remaining chalk particles and provide a sound surface base for the topcoat. In any event, clean the paint surface first to remove as much chalking paint as possible.

Painting Stucco

Paints are available that are designated for use over stucco. But, as you may have noticed, stucco that has been painted often peels, making an unattractive mess. The stucco/paint peeling problem is worst in areas where there are extreme (read cold) winter temperatures. Moisture passes from the house interior through the stucco exterior in cold weather, causing any paint to peel. So my advice is to check the local customs in your area for how to renew stucco, and follow the pro's lead.

If you live in the far west or south where winter moisture is not a problem (or even if you don't), use an acrylic emulsion paint such as Thorosheen

Use a clean, folded cloth as an applicator for applying dual-purpose ZAR Wood Stain and Sealer. Sand wood surface between coats to eliminate raised grain, dust. Photo courtesy UGL.

Use a spinner tool to spin residual paint out of paint brushes, rollers. Complete cleaning will make your paint tools last longer, save money. Author photo.

(Thoro System Products, 7800 N.W. 38th Street, Miami, FL 33166-6599) for painting stucco. Thorosheen lets the masonry "breathe" to reduce peeling problems. It can also be used for coating exterior or interior cement or cement block walls.

If you live in an area where moisture transfer in winter peels paint from wood siding and stucco, you can use a cement-base stucco finish called THORO STUCCO, made by the same company as Thorosheen. The cement-base material can be applied in any texture finish and is available in a variety of colors. Power wash the stucco surface to clean it, then use a stiff bristle brush to apply THORO STUCCO.

Log Home Exteriors

Following is advice from the National Association Of Home Builders on how to maintain and preserve log home exteriors.

Most logs for homes are first treated with zinc napthanate to control stain fungi, then dipped into sodium borate solution to protect the logs against insects or fungi. When the log house is erected the owner should follow a three-step maintenance procedure.

(1) Use a homemade cleaning solution to wash the logs. Dissolve 4 ounces of Savogran TSP-PF (phosphate-free) or low-phosphate detergent in a solution of one quart of chlorine bleach and three quarts of water (cleans about 250 square feet of logs). Cover any plants with plastic to protect them from the cleaner.

Wet the logs down with water from a garden hose. Use a garden sprayer to apply the cleaning solution and let the solution stand on the log surface for fifteen to thirty minutes, or until the discoloration begins to lift. Power wash the grime and solution away, using the washer at 500 pounds pressure. This procedure can be used on either older or new log homes to remove fungi, dirt, and air pollutants. Re-

apply the cleaner if necessary to be sure the logs are cleaned, then rinse and let dry before proceeding.

(2) When the logs are cleaned apply one or two coats of wood preservative. Preservatives available include Wolman Clear, Flood Seasonite, Sikkens Wood Preservative, and Chapman Wood Guard. Follow the log home dealer's instructions as well as the label instructions on your chosen preservative product.

(3) To preserve the natural log color use a transparent wood treatment such as Flood CWF or Aquatrol; Weatherall Log Guard; Wolman Raincoat; or Chapman Wood Guard. To add color without covering the wood grain use Olympic Semitransparent Stain, pigmented Wood Guard, pigmented Log Guard, or Wolman Raincoat with Natural Wood Toner.

Never use paint or varnish finishes on log homes, because any hard surface film will crack and peel as logs expand and contract from moisture changes.

Redwood and Cedar

Redwood and cedar sidings, in either rough-sawn or smooth finishes, are the premier choices for quality wood exteriors. During the past decade or more it has become popular to leave these wood sidings untreated, to age to a gray color. The problem is that air pollutants and mildew may turn the wood color so it grays unevenly, so that the wood discolors in splotches ranging from a light brown to black. This coating of grime and mildew can be removed using the same formula as above, for log siding, or use one of the wood cleaners advertised for cleaning decks, such as DEKSWOOD. However, if you decide to pressure-wash the siding, keep water pressures low, under 1,000 psi, to avoid damaging the siding surfaces. See the Exterior and Interior Finishing Charts, compiled by the California Redwood Association, for further directions.

To get a gray hue on wood siding and at the same

EXTERIOR FINISHES FOR REDWOOD

DESCRIPTION	USES	EFFECT	APPLICATION	MAINTENANCE
Clear Water Repellents with Mildewcide Clear finishes that modify weathering characteristics and let color and grain show through.	Certified Kiln Dried or air seasoned siding, fascia, trim, decks, fences, garden structures, commercial and industrial buildings. Finishes containing toxic mildewcides are not recommended for seating, tables, or interiors.	Minimize weather and mildew attack. Stabilize redwood's color at buckskin tan. Help eliminate redwood's natural darkening period. Areas exposed to direct sun and rain may eventually bleach to gray.	Apply with brush or roller. Lap marks and brushstrokes will not show through. Two coats recommended for new wood. For best results, coat sawn ends, backs, and edges before nailing in place. Read labels: Mildewcides may be toxic.	Reapplication may be required after old finish has lost its effectiveness. In humid or harsher climates, reapplication may be required every 18-24 months. Before applying, wood may be restored to its natural color.
Bleaching Oils Low maintenance, natural appearance with a gray-toned finish.	Certified Kiln Dried or air seasoned siding, fascia, trim, decks, fences, garden structures, commercial and industrial buildings. Finishes containing toxic mildewcides are not recommended for seating, tables, or interiors.	Provide for low maintenance and give redwood a uniformly gray or naturally weathered look.	Apply with brush or roller. Lap marks and brushstrokes may show through as many bleaches include gray pigment. Use one or two coats according to manufacturer's directions. Bleaching is aided by sunlight and moisture, so it may speed the process to periodically dampen surfaces with a fine spray from a garden hose.	Bleaching oils and stains provide nearly maintenance-free performance. Reapply finish only if wood begins to darken or bleaching is uneven. One refinish coat should be enough.
Semitransparent, or Lightly Pigmented Stains "Breathing" finishes available in a variety of semitransparent colors including several redwood hues. Oil-based stains are recommended.	Certified Kiln Dried or air seasoned siding, fascia, trim, decks, fences, garden structures, commercial and industrial buildings.	Provide color in a finish that lets wood breathe naturally. Semitransparent stains let the grain show through but present a uniform single color. The amount of pigment contained in stains will vary according to brand.	Apply with brush for best results, next best is a roller. Avoid drips and lap marks. Two coats usually required for new wood —follow manufacturer's directions.	Refinishing may be necessary every 3-5 years. Color in pigmented stains may wear away gradually after weathering. Light brushing with a bristle brush will help remove old finish in some spots. One refinish coat is usually enough.
Opaque Stains "Breathing" finishes available in a variety of opaque colors. Oil-based stains are recommended.	Certified Kiln Dried or air seasoned siding, fascia, trim, decks, fences, garden structures and furniture, commercial and industrial buildings.	Provide color in a finish that lets wood breathe naturally. Opaque stains will obscure the grain but highlight the texture and have an appearance more like paint.	For best results use a brush. The next best applicator is a roller. Avoid drips and lap marks. Two coats usually required for new wood —follow manufacturer's directions.	Refinishing may be necessary every 3-5 years. Color in pigmented stains may wear away gradually after weathering. Light brushing with a bristle brush will help remove old finish in some spots. One refinish coat is usually enough.
Paints Durable, attractive "non-breathing" finishes for traditional exteriors. Quality paints are generally worth the extra cost.	Certified Kiln Dried siding, fascia, trim, some garden structures and furniture, commercial and industrial buildings. Not recommended for decks and walking or seating surfaces. Note: For air-seasoned or unseasoned siding use a stain-blocking latex primer formulated for redwood.	Provide attractive colorful finishes which obscure grain and texture of the wood.	Apply with brush for best results, roller is next best applicator. Do not spray. One prime and two finish coats are recommended for new wood. Back-priming is advised. Use oil or alkyd resin base prime regardless of type of top coat. Latex top coat recommended.	Repaint one coat after most of old coat has weathered. Paint films that are too thick tend to peel and crack. Sand or scrub with stiff bristle brush. Paint and varnish removers may also be used. If sanding, countersink galvanized nail heads to protect their coating.

Courtesy of the California Redwood Association.

INTERIOR FINISHES FOR REDWOOD

DESCRIPTION	USES	EFFECT	APPLICATION	MAINTENANCE
Unfinished Unfinished redwood is suitable for areas requiring minimum cleaning such as ceilings. Wood may darken with time.	Light traffic areas, ceilings, walls, panels, and trim not cleaned often. Do not use in kitchens, bathrooms, or other areas exposed to moisture and grease.	Completely natural appearance. Wood may darken with time.		A finish may be applied at a later time if required.
Wax Natural appearance finish which highlights redwood's beauty.	All interior uses except kitchens and bathrooms.	Adds soft luster to redwood and touch-up is smooth, easy, and even. Applying wax over two coats of clear lacquer makes it easier to remove or paint over.	Apply with a soft cloth, rubbing with wood grain. On saw-textured surface, apply with stiff brush.	Wash with mild detergent, rinse with damp cloth. Remove grime with nonmetallic scouring pad. Restore appearance with new coat of wax; wipe off excess.
Alkyd Resin Sealers & Danish Oil Moderately durable finish with natural appearance.	All interior uses except bath rooms. Good for use on saw-textured surfaces.	These clear, flat penetrating sealers will darken redwood appreciably.	Two coats, brushed on.	Clean with damp cloth.
Clear Lacquer Film-forming finish for areas requiring minimum maintenance.	Ceilings, walls, dividers, trim, anywhere that needs only dry cleaning; not bathrooms, kitchens, or other areas requiring scrubbing.	Natural appearance with some protection from dirt. Although it forms a film, clear lacquer isn't glossy unless many coats are applied. Will darken wood slightly.	Apply by spraying (beware open flames) or brush on. Coat or two of wax over lacquer gives rich luster. Buff with soft cloth.	Clean with soft cloth dampened with turpentine, mineral spirits, or water. See maintenance suggestion under "Wax" for lacquer finishes topped with wax.
Alkyd Resin & Polyurethane Varnishes Clear protective finishes ideal for areas requiring scrubbing and heavy cleaning.	All interior uses on surfaced redwood. Multiple coats good for kitchens and bathrooms.	Provides flat, semi-gloss, or glossy textures, varnishes seal better than lacquers and withstand hard scrubbing. They darken and deepen woodtones and may show scratches.	Brush on two coats for most uses, up to six coats for kitchens and bathrooms. Let dry and sand lightly between coats.	Clean with soapy water and soft cloth. Or use turpentine or mineral spirits. Touch up scratches or nicks with tinted wax.
Pigmented Finishes Semitransparent or solid body stains or paints available in a variety of colors.	Any interior use. Protect stains from liquids, soiling, or frequent cleaning by covering with a clear finish or satin sealer (see "Stain and Clear Combinations").	Available in many colors. Stains may be preferred to paints because they only partially obscure redwood grain and texture.	Brush, roll, or spray. More coats mean deeper color effect. To emphasize grain or texture, apply one coat stain, wipe surface before dry. Use oil-base primers when painting new redwood.	Easy maintenance. Avoid heavy scrubbing that may smudge wood.
Stain and Clear Combinations Color stain is applied first, then a protective clear overcoat is applied. Stain provides color tone desired. Overcoats provide protection.	Same as "Pigmented Stains."	Same as "Pigmented Stains." Protect from grease, dirt, liquids with one coat of wax, lacquer, or varnish.	Follow maintenance instruction for whatever finish is used as the overcoat.	

Courtesy of the California Redwood Association.

time avoid the problems with uneven graying or discoloration, apply a bleaching oil. Bleaching oils will yield a natural appearance with a gray-tone finish, while preventing attack by grime and mildew.

Painting Aluminum Siding

Metal siding such as aluminum or steel is touted as being maintenance free, i.e., "never" needing painting. Aluminum siding of itself is corrosion-free, but the paint coating will degrade in time. Aluminum siding finish is usually warranted for twenty years or more, but the day will come when the siding will need repainting.

Most premium-quality acrylic latex house paints are also recommended for use on aluminum siding: check the label to be sure before selecting any particular product. Pittsburgh Paint, for example, not only recommends their exterior latex for use on aluminum, they also offer a full range of original siding colors, so you can repaint the siding in the exact same color as the original, if you wish. But first:

As mentioned earlier, use DEKSWOOD cleaner by the Flood Company to clean away dulled and chalked paint from the siding. Follow label directions for application of the cleaner. The result may be a dull but clean siding finish.

If the siding is clean but dull, and the old paint film is intact, try clearcoating the aluminum siding, using another Flood Company product called Penetrol (call 800-321-3444 if you can't locate these products). I tried this technique on my own aluminum siding and the results were remarkable. At worst, the Penetrol will make a good base coat for applying a new coat of paint. If only paint will renew your siding, use any major brand of acrylic latex paint, applied as per label instructions.

Staining Fiberglass Doors

One result of our concerns for energy conservation has been the development of energy-efficient doors. These doors are made of steel or fiberglass, with insulated cores. The doors not only conserve energy, they also resist swelling, warping, splitting, and sticking that are sometimes seen in wood doors.

The problem has been that these doors are often difficult to finish. Fiberglass doors may even have an embossed wood grain in the finish, but manufacturers have in the past recommended that you use artist's oil to stain the doors. Artist's oils are difficult to work with, plus being expensive: a door kit with artist's oil usually sells for about $30, while a new stain product, ZAR Wood Stain, costs about $3 for the average door. United Gilsonite Laboratories (UGL), maker of ZAR, also offers a wood graining tool to help you achieve an attractive grain pattern on the fiberglass doors (it works equally well on wood or metal doors). If your dealer cannot supply you, call (800) UGL-LABS for the name of a dealer near you.

EXTERIOR STAINS

On wood siding or outdoor structures, exterior stains can provide an attractive alternative to paint. For most applications, such as over redwood, oil-base stains are recommended.

Stains are products that consist mainly of vehicle, with low percentages of pigment. The pigments may be just enough to lend a tint of color to the protective stain, without concealing the grain and character of the wood. Semitransparent stains, sometimes called Lightly Pigmented Stains, are available in a variety of colors plus several redwood hues. These are called "breathing" finishes and penetrate and protect the wood while avoiding the formation of any surface film that might block moisture migration from the siding. Also offered are opaque stains, which have many of the same protective characteristics mentioned but have more pigment than semitransparent stains.

ENVIRONMENTAL CONSIDERATIONS

The development of water- or latex-base paints has coincided with the recent and overdue concern for our environment. Using latex paints not only eliminates the problems of VOCs or Volatile Organic Compounds, it eliminates the need for using many of the sundry chemicals that are necessary when using oil or alkyd finishes. Using latex base paints eliminates a whole array of solvents, thinners, and cleaners, so it is well to use latex paints for any project for which a latex paint will do. As latex paint chemistry has advanced, latexes are recommended for almost any application. There was a time when problem surfaces almost immediately dictated the use of oil-base paints, but no more. Whether you are painting aluminum siding, chalking paint, concrete, or concrete floors, latex paint is the preferred choice.

For exterior use, I use an oil-base deck finish named Cuprinol. I've found it to be superior to anything I've used for durability on the deck surface. Likewise, the California Redwood Association recommends oil-base stains for redwood. Check the label on any oil-base products you choose, to be sure they meet the standards for VOC emissions.

Whatever paint and stain products you use, read label instructions carefully and follow guidelines for safe disposal. Try to use up any product you buy, perhaps by giving a wall an extra coat of paint or by using leftover paints in closets. When you've used up all the material, open the paint can and let any leftovers harden in the can, then dispose of the can in the trash. You should, of course, check with your own local government for advice on how to dispose of any hazardous waste materials.

PAINTING TOOLS

To ensure a better paint job, choose professional-quality tools. As we mentioned in Chapter 1: Tools, when you consider the difference in price between good/better/best hand tools you are often talking about a difference of just a few dollars. While you usually don't pay much more for a quality tool, the difference in results can be striking. This is especially true when choosing paint tools.

9.
Caulks and Patchers

Not many years ago the caulks available to home-owners were limited to oil-base or asphaltic products. The products were messy to apply and spread, and they hardened and cracked as they cured, so that renewing caulking was a seasonal project. Patching materials for use on roofing, asphalt, or concrete were available only in bulk, in cans of one quart or more, and were messy to apply and prone to early failure. Patching concrete involved mixing sand and Portland cement together, again a messy business. The result was often a patch failure, as the new concrete failed to bond with the old. Left-over patching materials often hardened in the containers, so anything that was not used up immediately was wasted.

Advances in chemistry have resulted in the production of more durable caulks and patching products for the homeowner. Not only is a wider selection of patching products now available, but durability has improved to the point that caulks are now offered with twenty-five-year warranties. Silicone and acrylic latex caulks are "elastomeric," meaning they remain elastic after curing, rather than becoming brittle as oil-base caulks do. This elastic property means that the caulks remain flexible for long periods of time and do not crack as the building materials swell and shrink with temperature and humidity changes.

APPLICATION TOOLS

Most of these caulk and patch products are packaged in caulk tubes and can be applied with inexpensive caulking guns. Some, such as the tub and tile caulks, are available in squeeze tubes and require no tools for application. These squeeze-caulks are especially good for apartment dwellers who want to seal grimy cracks between the tub/tile line, but have no room for storing caulking guns and other tools.

The nozzles on caulk tubes often are marked at cutoff points, so you can choose the right bead diameter for applying the caulk, depending on the width of the crack to be filled. Don't just squeeze the handle on the caulk gun to start the caulk flowing. To avoid a mess, first use a piece of wire or a carpenter's awl to puncture the sealing membrane inside the nozzle.

The most common caulk tube size is the 10-ounce tube, but quart-size tubes and caulk guns are available at most professional tool outlets. A 10-ounce

DAP 230 Sealant offers good adhesion, long-term durability, and resistance to mold or mildew. Photo courtesy USG.

New caulk technology makes possible the long-life acrylic latex-plus-silicone product shown. Use twenty-five-year products to reduce maintenance duties plus reducing waste flow. Photo courtesy UGL.

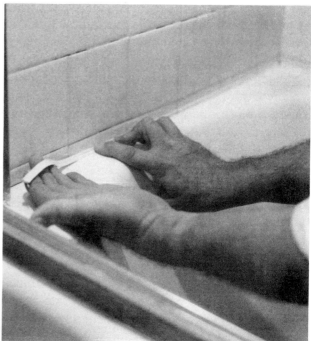

Pre-formed tub/tile caulk from 3M offers a cove-shaped adhesive caulk that can be applied without using tools. Author photo.

tube will fill about 25 linear feet of crack that is ¼-inch wide, and will fill up to 100 linear feet with a ⅛-inch wide bead. Try to plan your caulk or patch job to use up all the product in the caulk tube, because it is difficult to store any caulk or patch product once the nozzle has been cut and air has reached the material. The best tip to reseal a caulk tube is to use an oversized electrical wire nut screwed on the nozzle of the caulk tube, but any such attempt will seal the tube only for a short period of time. Air that has already entered the nozzle will cause the caulk to harden in the nozzle tip.

You will need a razor knife or other sharp knife to cut the nozzle end of the caulk tube. You may use a Popsicle stick or a plastic spoon, dipped in the appropriate solvent, to smooth the caulk or patch product. Wet the tool in water for smoothing latex or silicone products; use mineral spirits as a solvent for smoothing asphaltic or oil-based products such as blacktop patchers or roofing mastics.

CAULKS

Cheaper oil-base caulks will not last as long as latex or silicone caulks, and they are more expensive in the long run. The difference in initial cost between a quality caulk and the cheapest caulk is only a dollar or two per tube. Buying a quality caulk product will save money and time in the long run, and will eliminate those frequent caulk repair sessions. Especially for caulking at high gables or for patching on high, steep roofs where ladder work is required, use the longest-lasting caulk product you can find to eliminate frequent repairs.

Following is a brief review of the types of caulks available. Remember, price is almost irrelevant when you are thinking about caulk products, because the total amount of product needed is small.

- Acrylic latex caulks are easy to apply, and you can clean tools or hands with water.

Most latex caulks are available in a wide variety of colors, or they can be painted over within a matter of several hours. Some acrylic latex caulks, such as UGL's Lasticaulk™ also contain silicones for long life and good extended flexibility. Lasticaulk is available in white, clear, or almond; some caulks feature other colors.

- Silicone caulks are a bit more expensive than latexes but are easy to apply and are very durable: many silicones have warranties up to twenty-five years. Check the label to find whether the silicone caulk can be painted. Some silicone caulks may require priming of surfaces prior to caulking; check the label directions for your particular product. Consider using these more durable caulks for those hard-to-reach places that must be reached via a ladder, to save having to do frequent repairs.

- Tub/tile caulks are acrylic latex products and should be used to seal the joint where bathtub and ceramic tile meet. Tub/tile caulks remain flexible after curing and do not crack as they age, as brittle caulks or tile grout will. Check to be sure the caulk is resistant to mildew for added protection in this damp and vulnerable area. To remove dirt and soap scum, and to provide a clean surface for the caulk to adhere to, clean the tub and tile area with ordinary rubbing (isopropyl) alcohol prior to caulking. Let the caulk cure for forty-eight hours before running the shower and wetting the caulk.

- Adhesive caulks such as Polyseamseal™ by Darworth Co. provide good adhesion to most materials and are recommended for use in areas of high water exposure, such as in bathrooms or on boats. Superior adhesive properties let you use the product to reset loose ceramic tiles, seal around glass

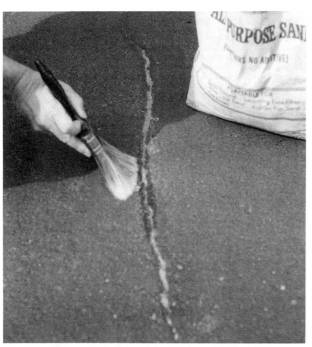

Pre-fill wide or deep cracks with sand to avoid wasting asphalt patcher.

Use an asphalt patching product to seal blacktop drive against water entry, possible damage.

Caulk-type concrete repair products eliminate chiseling out cracks. Just clean debris from crack and apply the concrete patcher, following label directions. Author photo.

or portholes, secure and seal countertops and sink rims. Clean up with water before the caulk sets.

- Butyl caulk is made from butyl rubber and is a durable all-purpose caulk. Use for chimneys, skylights, gutters, or boats — wherever a waterproof rubber sealant is needed to guard against water entry.

The above caulks will perform for most caulk jobs around the home. Stay away from cheap oil-base caulk products that will fail prematurely. Check label instructions for application: perform cleaning and/or sealing of the caulk surface as directed. It's a good practice to clean and caulk all cracks in siding, or around windows and doors, before pressure-washing the house exterior. Caulking before power washing will seal cracks to prevent water from entering between cracks and causing rot or paint peeling.

TUBE PATCHERS

Patching products available in caulk tubes eliminate messy mixing and permit controlled application and placement of the patching product. Tube patchers are available for patching roofing, concrete, and asphalt. Using these adhesive patching products saves labor, because no undercutting or chiseling of cracks in concrete or asphalt is necessary. Unlike cement-based patching products, tube-type patch products are adhesive and will stick to any clean, properly prepared surface.

Among the latest developments are latex-base patchers for both concrete and asphalt. Latex products give off no polluting vapors and do not require volatile solvents for cleanup. As concern for the environment rises there is increased demand for home repair products that clean up with water and eliminate volatile organic compounds (VOCs).

Tips for using caulks and patchers include:

- To save money on patch products and to reduce the amount of caulk or patcher needed, fill deep or wide cracks with sand, plumber's oakum, or fiberglass insulation to within ¼ inch of the surface. Then fill the remaining ¼-inch gap with caulk or patcher and smooth.

- Clean and prepare the surface to be caulked, following product label directions. Use a blower or shop vacuum to remove any dirt or foreign matter from the crack. Apply and smooth the caulk per instructions. Heed label information regarding cure time and painting.

- To limit caulk or patch area, and to make a neat repair, use masking tape along the caulk or patch application area. Use the appropriate solvent to clean up any smears or spills, and to clean tools.

- When you are applying roofing cement, press a layer of fine sand into the cement after placing it. The sand will help the roofing cement resist drying out and cracking from exposure to the sun's ultraviolet rays.

- Plan your work carefully and try to use the entire contents of the caulk tube, to avoid dried-up and wasted caulk or patcher. It is very difficult to save patching products once air has reached the material in the nozzle.

- Use latex-base patchers and caulks where they are available, because latex or water-base materials are less polluting. Use all the product in the tube and dispose of the empty tube per the label instructions, or check with your local EPA office for advice on how to dispose of the container safely.

10.
Masonry Repair Products

Homeowner repair of concrete and masonry was once nearly impossible. Concrete of itself has no adhesive properties and will not adhere to old concrete when applied in thin layers or patches. Plus, masonry that is damaged—a broken edge on a step, for example—will usually be soiled with dirt. The dirt interferes with the patching process by causing a poor bond between the old concrete and the new patching material. Cement and sand were once packaged in large quantities for professional use only: if one needed 10 pounds of cement to make a repair, what can one do with 84 pounds of cement leftovers from a 94-pound bag? Too often, the leftover cement would harden in the bag as it absorbed moisture from the air, and would end up wasted.

Today, packaged masonry and concrete repair products contain all the needed ingredients, all carefully weighed and blended to the correct proportions. Latex bonding agents are included in the mix, or packaged in a separate can in a kit, and the bonding agents make the concrete patcher "sticky" enough to bond to the old concrete. The patching kit is packaged in a plastic pail that serves as a mixing pail and can be discarded in the trash without cleaning when the job is finished.

Also available are bagged products that have brand names such as Sakrete and Quikrete, which contain cement, sand, and gravel mixed in the proper proportion and are intended to eliminate the mess of home mixing. All you have to add is water. In fact, if you are pouring concrete piers or supporting fence posts below ground, you can dump in many of these products dry and let the ground moisture set the material, or pour a little water in the hole on top of the dry mix. If you must mix the concrete patch product with water, pour the dry mix in a wheelbarrow or a 5-gallon plastic pail and mix it with a garden hoe or trowel. Or buy a mixing bit from a wallboard tool store and chuck the mixing bit into a ½-inch drill to mix concrete or asphalt patchers.

If you are building a large concrete project such as a driveway or patio slab, you may want to rent a cement mixer and do your own mixing. The alternative to using a portable mixer would be to order ready-mix concrete delivered by a truck. Before making the decision to mix your own concrete you should consider the advantages of having the material mixed in a truck, or "in transit." The truck mix will be properly proportioned in the amounts of Portland cement, sand, and gravel. It will have the

To ensure that cement repair will bond firmly to the old concrete, apply a coat of latex concrete bonding adhesive to the entire surface. Author photo.

Use a trowel to apply a coat of cement over the entire area. Finish with a second coat of cement or stucco. Author photo.

If the concrete blocks also have holes to be filled, use concrete nails to fasten wire lath over the block. Author photo.

To repair a damaged step, first use a wire brush to clean away loose concrete. Author photo.

Apply latex bonding liquid to the patch area. Author photo.

Mix concrete patcher in a plastic or paper pail. Apply concrete to patch area, to begin repair sequence. Apply as much repair material as will stand without a form to hold it. Author photo.

Nail together a 90-degree corner form, using scrap lumber. Position the form around the corner of the step, using duct tape to hold the form in position. Fill the form with cement and smooth with a knife. Author photo.

When the cement begins to set, but before it is completely hardened, remove the wooden form from the corner. Use a wet paint brush to smooth the sides of the repair. Author photo.

Use a wire brush to clean efflorescence and dirt from the concrete surface. Photo courtesy UGL.

Patch any cracks or holes in the wall using a hydraulic cement. Mix concrete repair products in throwaway plastic or paper mixing pails. Photo courtesy UGL.

Clean any floor-level cracks using a masonry chisel and hammer. Wear eye goggles when driving a chisel or any tool. Photo courtesy UGL.

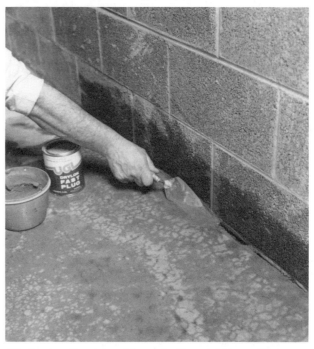

Mix hydraulic cement in a plastic container. Use a pointing trowel to fill the crack, troweling the cement into a cove shape between the wall and the floor. Photo courtesy UGL.

Apply a masonry waterproofer to the entire wall. If the wall has been subject to wetness, first apply a coat of waterproofer about 2 feet high up the wall. Let dry, then recoat the entire wall for double protection at the wall bottom. Photo courtesy UGL.

Any concrete surface to be patched should be clean and free from peeling or efflorescence. Cement patcher will not bond to a dirty or unsound surface. Photo courtesy Sears.

proper "slump" or consistency, and there is no mess from on-site mixing. And the truck will direct a chute over the formed project and place the concrete for you. This placement is no small thing: we are talking of mixing, moving, and spreading tons of concrete. That's a lot of work to save a few bucks.

If you decide to mix your own concrete, you can buy cement in 94-pound bags (1 cubic foot), and buy sand in bags or in bulk from masonry supply firms or gravel dealers. If you choose to do so, the mixing formula for concrete is easy as 1-2-3: mix 1 part of Portland cement, 2 parts of sand, and 3 parts of gravel, with enough water to make a firm mudball when you grip a handful (note that the consistency of the mix will vary: more water will be needed for spreading a concrete slab, or for working in hot weather when a thick, dry mix will set quickly and be difficult to trowel). Always add water sparingly: keep in mind that bulk sand may have a high water content, so less water will be required than with dry sand.

Masonry patching requires the appropriate patch material—depending on whether you are patching a hole or a crack in masonry—plus a stick or mixing bit (for your drill) if mixing is required. For caulk-tube repair products, you will need a caulk gun for applying the patcher, a razor knife for cutting the nozzle tip, and a Popsicle stick or plastic spoon for smoothing the patch material. You will also need the appropriate solvent: water for cleaning up latex patchers, and mineral spirits for cleaning up asphaltic or oil-base products. You will also need a selection of small paint scrapers or trowels to apply and smooth holes or patches in damaged concrete.

PATCHING CRACKS

Most narrow cracks in concrete — up to ¼-inch wide—can be successfully patched using the caulk-tube masonry patchers. Check the color of the patcher: some concrete patchers are white and will stand out against the natural gray color of the concrete. Brands we've used successfully include DAP and UGL. Remember, to reduce the amount of patch roduct needed and control the cost of the repair, fill any crack with sand or fiberglass insulation, up to about ¼ inch from the surface, then complete the repair with patching compound. Follow label directions and observe temperature and other label information to ensure a successful repair.

If the crack is in a basement wall or floor, and water is entering through the crack, first try to adjust rain gutters and the grade of the soil to divert water away from the basement wall. It is easier to divert water away from the foundation, via rain gutters and improved grade or lawn slope, than to make any foundation wall waterproof. When you have dried up the water as much as possible, clean the crack so it is free of debris and fill the crack with a fast-setting hydraulic cement such as UGL's Drylok Fast Plug. The crack area must be clean but need not be dry when you apply the patcher. This product must be mixed with water, because the chemistry is such that it cannot be offered as a ready-mix product. When the concrete patcher sets, seal the leak area with a concrete waterproofing product.

PATCHING HOLES IN CONCRETE

For patching holes or other damage in concrete, you must use a latex concrete bonder to ensure a bond between the old and new concrete surfaces. You can buy the product in plastic bottles, with names such as UGL's Drylok Latex Bonding Agent or Quikrete Concrete Bonding Adhesive. The latex bonder will also be used on the home interior to bond new plaster patches to old plaster.

If you buy a concrete patcher kit in a plastic pail, check the label to see if the latex bonding agent is included. If it is not, buy the bonding agent separately and add it to the concrete mix as per directions. In addition to adding the latex bonder to the concrete mix, use a paint brush to coat the old concrete surfaces you want to repair. Let the bonder tack slightly, but not set completely, before applying the patching material.

CONCRETE/MASONRY SEALERS

Most concrete and masonry surfaces should be sealed, although a properly constructed brick wall should shed the rain and avoid freeze damage. However, even brick construction may suffer from freeze damage in cold climates, if left unsealed. Brick window sills, for example, sometimes will spall if snow accumulates on them and freezes there. Check with dealers or masonry contractors in your area to learn local wisdom for sealing brick, masonry, or concrete. The practices vary by location and by climate: sealing exterior concrete is especially important in areas that are subject to extreme winter temperatures, because water may penetrate a concrete surface and expand and damage the concrete when the water freezes.

A wide selection of concrete and masonry sealers is available. Read the label or check with the dealer to be sure you buy the right sealer. Some sealers, such as silicone sealers, are intended for use only on vertical masonry surfaces such as walls, and are not to be used to seal a wear surface such as a concrete garage floor or driveway. Other clear masonry sealers are effective when used on any exterior surface, including driveways, and can be excellent when used as primers before applying concrete floor paint.

Clear acrylic sealers can be used to protect brick, stucco, terrazzo, concrete, and other masonry surfaces and should be used as a primer for applying

latex masonry paints. Explain what you want to use the primer for, and ask your dealer to help you select the appropriate product for your job.

MASONRY WATERPROOFING PAINTS

It is asking much from a paint or masonry sealer to keep out standing water. If you have a basement water problem you should consider the concrete waterproofer as the last line of defense against water entry, not the primary barrier. The first step is to correct any grade problems or lack of effective rain gutters, so water is diverted away from the concrete wall. Professionals such as the National Association of Home Builders agree that 95 percent of basement water problems could easily be prevented by proper lawn grading, an effective rain gutter system, and a coat of waterproofer on the concrete wall. Remember, in a wet basement, cracks in concrete basement walls are not the problem; water entry is the problem. If you divert surface water away from the walls the cracks will be dry, but if you only patch the cracks the water is still present and still a problem.

Once you have diverted water away from the basement walls by correcting poor drainage and installing rain gutters, apply a coat or two of waterproofer to the inside of the walls. Top manufacturers to look for include names such as UGL (United Gilsonite Laboratories, makers of Drylok Masonry Waterproofer) and Thoro System Products' Thoroseal. Thoro also makes a wide array of concrete repair and sealing products. Another superior brand name is United States Gypsum (USG), manufacturers of a wide variety of concrete, wallboard, and plaster repair products.

11. Roofing

More than 80 percent of the homes in the U.S. have asphalt roof shingles or roll roofing. Another 10 percent of roofs are wood, usually cedar, and are either hand-split shakes or shingles.

Roofing a house requires a broad array of skills and knowledge, as well as special scaffolding and ladders to reach the work. The work is heavy and involves a considerable risk of injury because of the heights and climbing involved. Many manufacturers of asphalt shingles discourage homeowners from attempting roofing work because of the consumer liability laws. Still, some shingle manufacturers have moved into the do-it-yourself market because of the number of homeowners who are physically capable of doing the work and who will attempt it in any case.

The decision of whether to attempt your own roofing work is entirely an individual one, and should take into account your own experience level, your physical health and strength, and your ability to work at heights. I once knew an airline pilot who was afraid of heights and would not climb a ladder to change his own storm windows. Obviously, this person was not a candidate for doing his own roofing.

If you don't mind climbing, you can at least do periodic cleaning and maintenance on your asphalt or wood shingle roof. Advice on roof maintenance will be given at the end of this chapter.

A minority of houses, a total of about 10 percent, have roofs of metal, slate, or tile. Because slate, tile, and metal roofs require special installation tools and techniques and professional installation and repair, they are beyond the scope of most do-it-yourself homeowners.

WHEN TO REROOF

Inspect your roof each spring and fall to check for storm damage. If you cannot climb on the roof, use a pair of binoculars to take a close look at the entire roof structure. Check rain gutters to be sure they were not loosened by ice at the eaves. Replace or repair any windblown shingles; apply roof mastic around any chimney or vent flashings and valleys;

and check in gutters and downspouts for signs of loose shingle granules. As the asphalt shingles dry out, the ceramic granules will come loose and will wash down the roof deck. A buildup of shingle granules, or brittle, broken, or curled shingles is a sure sign that the roof is due for replacement. Most older shingle roofs were installed using shingles with a 15 to 20 year warranty, so if you know the year the roof was installed you can get a good idea whether the roof may be about due for replacement.

SHOULD YOU SHINGLE?

Shingles shed water but do not waterproof. If properly applied, on a roof with sufficient slope or pitch, the overlapping shingles let the water run harmlessly off the roof, without penetrating into the house. But you should never apply asphalt shingles over a roof that has less than a $2/12$ slope, meaning a slope of 2 inches for each 12 inches of lateral run. Do not confuse the roofing terms "slope" and "pitch." The pitch of a roof is the ratio of the vertical rise to double the horizontal run and is shown as a fraction. For example, a roof that has a 4-inch rise per foot of horizontal run would have a $4/12$ slope, but would have a $1/6$ pitch ($4/24 = 1/6$).

Should you use asphalt shingles on a roof? A basic rule of thumb is: if you can see the roof from ground level, it is steep enough to have shingles; but if the roof is too flat to be seen from ground level you should install either roll or built-up roofing. To check the slope, place the top end of a 2-foot carpenter's level against the roof, and raise the lower end of the level until the bubble is centered in the dial. Then use a rule to measure from the bottom edge of the level's end down to the roof deck. At the lower or outside end of the level, the distance between the bottom edge of the level and the roof should be 4 inches or more (2 inches of slope per foot x 2 feet of run). If the roof slope is marginal — 2 inches/foot ($2/12$) or less — use roll

roofing or have a pitch and gravel built-up roof installed. For roof slopes of between 2 and 4 inches/foot, you can use shingles, being careful to follow the manufacturer's installation instructions for low slope roofs. If your roof slope is $4/12$ or more, you may apply shingles as per manufacturer's instructions, without fear of leaks due to poor slope or water runoff.

SELECTING THE SHINGLES

Because they cover a large part of the exterior of the house, the color and appearance of the shingles are of primary importance to the consumer. Asphalt shingles are available in a wide variety of colors plus wood tones. The most common type, the 3-tab shingle, may have a warranty of 15 to 35 years, depending on its construction. Increased asphalt shingle life is due chiefly to two factors. The shingles have a fiberglass mat base that is more durable than the old felt shingle base, and ceramic shingle granules have replaced the old gravel granules to help protect the shingles from the sun's destructive ultraviolet rays. It is the sun's heat and ultraviolet rays that destroy asphalt shingles.

Shingles are bought and installed on a basis of "cost per square," and weight per square. A square of shingles is enough shingles to cover 100 square feet of roof (there are three bundles of shingles per square, or $33 1/3$ sq. ft. to the bundle). Weight per square is an indication of shingle quality: heavier shingles contain more asphalt per square foot, and so are heavier-duty. A common weight for 3-tab asphalt shingles is 235 pounds per square (shipping weight).

To find the annual cost of the shingles divide the total material cost by the number of years of warranty. For example, if shingles enough to cover your roof cost $2,500, with a 25-year warranty, the annual cost of the shingles would be $2,500/25 = $100 per year.

Check warranty information carefully. Most shingle warranties are not transferable, so if you sell your newly-shingled house the warranty cannot be transferred to the new owner, and the warranty lapses with the house sale. Also, look for a warranty that covers both materials and labor costs: some warranties cover the shingle cost only. In this case, if the shingles alone cost $2,000 and failed in half the warranty period, ten years for example, you might be looking at a $1,000 warranty payment to cover an inflated replacement roof cost of $4,000 for labor and materials. The best bet is to buy shingles with a recognized manufacturer's name on the label, and then narrow your selection on the basis of the warranties offered.

ACCESSORY MATERIALS

If you are doing a tear-down, or stripping the shingles down to the bare sheathing of the roof deck, this is a fine time to upgrade attic ventilation and rain gutters. The best attic ventilation to have is continuous venting at the eaves and at the roof ridge. With this ventilation system, cool air is drawn in at the eaves and warmed as it moves across the insulation or attic floor, and the warmed air rises. As the warmed attic air rises it flows out of the attic through the ridge vents, carrying any moisture in the attic outside. This cool air creates a vacuum behind it as it is heated, rises, and exits, and the vacuum thus created will pull in cool air through the eave vents. This natural air flow is called the "chimney effect" and is necessary to control attic moisture levels and relieve attic heat buildup. The best time to upgrade attic ventilation is when you are reroofing. Ask your dealer to suggest a brand of continuous ridge and soffit venting.

In addition to the shingles, you will need a number of accessory materials. First, you will need to buy roof underlayment, usually referred to as "15 pound felt," which is a roll material made of felt saturated with asphalt. This underlayment is rolled down on the bare roof sheathing and stapled in place, so the sheets overlap by about 2 inches. The underlayment serves several purposes: it protects the roof deck or sheathing, and the house interior, from rain while the reroofing is going on. The underlayment also provides a secondary barrier to the finished shingle roof, and ensures against windblown rain entering under the shingles. Be sure to use 15-pound felt underlayment, or its equivalent: do not install any material that might be a vapor barrier. A material that acts as a barrier to moisture passage will trap any leaked moisture or frost between the shingles and the roof deck.

You will also need valley flashing. Valley flashing in the past was made of galvanized sheet metal. In time the galvanized finish (zinc) weathered away, and the valley flashing rusted, so it leaked and stained the shingles. Today, most roofers are using aluminum valley flashing. The aluminum flashing is resistant to corrosion, and it is pre-finished both for visual appeal and for weather protection. Also, buy new metal flashing sleeves to fit over the chimney stack and plumbing vent pipes.

In colder climates where winter temperatures fall below 0° F, your building code may require that you install eave flashing. In some states in the northeast, such as Pennsylvania, a wide strip of aluminum flashing is installed at the roof eaves so that the sun, warming the metal, will melt ice and prevent ice dams from forming. In other areas a double layer of felt underlayment is installed at the roof edge to ensure against ice melting and running under the shingles. Usually this second layer of underlayment is installed so it extends at least 1 foot (12 inches) past the edge of the exterior walls on roofs with 4/12 or greater slope, and 2 feet (24 inches) past the exterior wall on low-slope roofs.

To prevent water damage at the edge of the roof, a metal drip edge is installed. The metal drip edge is intended to ensure that water that runs to the eave will drip off, not bead up and run back under the soffits or eaves.

You will also need some roofing cement to glue down shingle corners and seal any joints between roof shingles and valleys or flashings. Buy the roof cement in caulk tubes for easy, no-mess application. Buy extra tubes so you don't run out: most dealers will let you return unused, unopened tubes of roof cement.

You will need galvanized shingle nails. Your dealer can help you figure the quantity or number of pounds of nails you will need, based on the size of your roof, in squares or in hundreds of square feet.

TIP: if you are shingling over a clean deck, where the old layer of shingles has been removed, you can use 1½-inch nails. If you are reroofing over one layer of old shingles you should buy 2-inch roofing nails, to penetrate through the extra layers of shingles.

A recent consumer article talked about roofing and cautioned that a third layer of shingles would add too much weight on the rafters to be safe. Actually, most building codes (all codes that we are aware of) let you re-shingle over your first roof, but when you already have two layers of shingles on the roof you must tear down or remove the old roofing, down to the bare roof deck, and start anew: you cannot have three layers of shingles on the roof. Most such code prohibitions are based on common sense: the fire hazard of three layers of shingles, the difficulty in finding a leak in so thick a roof, and the danger of damaging the top shingles when walking and working over so many layers of shingles are all reasons not to apply more than two layers of shingles.

If you decide to reroof and do the work yourself, and you are removing the old roofing, call your trash collector and rent a dumpster. Have the dumpster set close enough to the house that you can throw the old shingles directly off the roof and into the dumpster, to avoid making a mess on the lawn and having to handle the debris twice. After finishing the job, drag a strong magnet on the lawn around the perimeter of the house to pick up any stray roofing nails. Stray nails may be picked up by a power lawn mower and thrown with dangerous force. Such projectiles are an injury hazard to the mower operator or anyone on the lawn, so try to avoid dropping any nails on the lawn.

To remove old shingles, use a 4-tine garden fork to pry under the edge of a shingle course or row. This will lift a large number of shingles at a single pass, and will remove most of the shingle nails at the same time. I have seen a pair of workmen remove the entire shingle load off a roof in a half-day effort, using the garden forks.

After you have the roof clean and the underlayment stapled in place, have the shingles delivered. Don't try to save delivery charges by hauling the shingles yourself: material dealers have elevators on their delivery trucks that will lift the shingles to the roof, saving you the effort of hauling the heavy shingles up a ladder. Getting the shingles on the roof is half the job, so take advantage of this special equipment and save yourself a lot of work.

Order enough shingles so you will have at least one bundle left over. These leftover shingles will ensure that you have matching shingles if the roof is damaged. I have even known people to open a bundle of shingles and lay shingles on the roof of a storage shed, so they would weather and age to match the roof shingles on the house if replacement was necessary. This precaution, while it may be a bit extreme, will avoid the problem of shingle repairs with new shingles that stand out so prominently against the aged shingles on a patched or repaired roof.

ROOF MAINTENANCE AND REPAIR

Roofing is a kind of "out of sight, out of mind" material, and many people ignore a roof as long as it is not leaking. There are, however, steps you can take to ensure that you get all the life your roof was designed to deliver.

First, keep the roof deck clean and dry. This means washing the roof occasionally to remove any twigs, leaves, or other debris from the joints or keyways between the shingles. Water that is trapped on a roof deck encourages dirt to accumulate and mildew spores to grow. Use a hose nozzle or a pressure washer to clean the roof deck. Companies that do cleaning will power wash the roof for you, if you choose not to do the work yourself.

Trim any tree limbs that overhang your roof. This is necessary to avoid damage from wind-blown limbs, and to let sunshine reach the roofing. At the least, trim tree limbs to thin them so the sun can dry the roof. Roof shingles that are perpetually shaded develop moss and mildew that will ruin the appearance of the roof and shorten the life of the shingles.

Do not climb or walk on a roof when the weather is very hot or very cold. In hot weather the asphalt shingles may soften to the extent that you will actually remove part of the asphalt on your shoes. Walking on an asphalt roof in cold weather may crack shingles that are cold and brittle. Let roof work wait until the temperature is between 50° and 80° F.

Keep in mind too that asphalt shingles are "self-sealing"; they have a strip of shingle adhesive on the bottom edge. This shingle adhesive is softened by the sun and causes the shingles to seal to the shingles below them. If the shingles are applied in cold weather and the protective strip that covers the shingle adhesive is removed, the adhesive may be too cold to stick to the shingle course below. The unsealed shingles will then become windblown in a storm and may be torn from the roof.

Inspect the roof in spring and fall to check for seasonal storm damage. Repair or replace damaged shingles. To replace missing or damaged shingles, lift up the old shingles and reach underneath with a small prybar to remove the shingle remnant and the old nails. Then insert the replacement shingle, holding the shingles above it, and renail the new shingle. Cover the nail heads with a spot of roof cement and press the shingle firmly in place against the shingle(s) below.

WOOD ROOFS

Wood shingle or shake roofs are very attractive and are a common choice for houses that have rustic wood siding. General maintenance instructions for wood roofs are about the same as for maintaining asphalt roofs. But because of the danger of wood rot from trapped moisture, it is even more important to clean the all-wood roof deck occasionally to remove leaves, twigs, and other debris that might trap moisture in the keyways between the shingles or shakes.

Also important for wood roofs is to be sure the roof deck gets sunlight to dry it. Once, wood shakes and shingles were laid over sleepers or boards spaced far apart, not laid over a solid wood roof sheathing such as plywood. This method of installation allowed the wood to dry both from above and from below. Laying wood shakes or shingles over a solid wood roof sheathing will trap any moisture between the shingles and the sheathing, and the shingles or shakes will quickly decay from wood rot. Thin tree branches so that sunlight can penetrate and dry the wood roof.

Wood roofs that are not permitted to dry are also subject to attack from moss or fungus. This is a particular problem in areas of high rainfall and year-round moderate temperatures where such growths are active all year. Northern California, Oregon, and Washington are states where moss growth is severe on wood roofs.

If you have a problem with existing moss or fungus growth, your roofing contractor can pressure-wash or brush the roof to remove present growth, then apply a chemical that will retard future growth.

If you prefer not to use chemicals, or you want to attack the moss/fungus problem yourself, first clean away the old growth. Then nail a product called Z-STOP at the ridges and on the lower side of chimneys or other objects that interfere with roof water flow. Z-STOP is a strip of zinc, 2½ inches wide, that can be nailed in place along the ridges of the roof. As rain falls on the metal it washes a small amount of zinc down the shingles, and the zinc will kill the moss or fungus. Look for Z-STOP at your home center, or contact the manufacturer for the name of a dealer near you. Z-STOP is made by: WESPAC, P.O. Box 46337, Seattle, WA 98146.

ROOFING TIPS

Climbing ladders and walking on roofs is a dangerous business. Not only are you working at a height, you are carrying heavy materials and/or sharp tools. Be sure you assess your own physical capabilities before considering roof work.

- Be sure the ladders you are using are strong enough to carry both your weight and the weight of any materials you are carrying. Cheap household ladders are not designed to carry a total weight of more than 200 pounds. Rent or borrow commercial-grade ladders.

- Wear rubber-soled work shoes or over-the-ankle boots when climbing and walking on roofs. The rubber (or crepe) soles prevent damage to roof shingles and are more slip-proof to help prevent falls.

- Don't climb with your hands full of tools. Place hand tools in a 5-gallon plastic pail, attach a length of clothesline or other rope,

and carry the end of the rope up the ladder to the roof. Then use the rope to hoist the pail of tools up on the roof.

- If you are cutting flashing, shingles, or shingle underlayment, throw scraps off the roof immediately. Scraps of shingle or metal flashing become toboggans when you step on them, and you can slide off a roof. Keep the roof deck clean to avoid falls.

- Wear tight-weave canvas work pants, such as jeans, to protect legs from roof cement and nails. Do not wear shorts or cutoffs on a roof.

- Wear eye goggles when driving shingle nails or any nails. Wash hands before eating, drinking, or smoking.

- Clean hammer heads and other tools frequently when working with roofing cement. A hammer face that is covered with roofing cement may slip off the nail and damage the shingle or injure the worker.

- Cutting the granules on shingles will quickly dull your knife blade. Dull blades cause accidents when you try to force the knife through the material. Replace the blade in your razor knife frequently to be sure it is sharp.

- Ask the dealer to deliver new shingles on the roof. Most often, the truck driver will place the shingle bundles on the elevator, but you (or another workman) must be on the roof to remove the bundles from the elevator and position them on the roof.

- If roofing in warm weather, work early and late, or during the coolest part of the day. If temperatures are above 80° F, you should delay roofing work until cooler weather so you won't damage the shingles.

- Never step back to admire your work.

12.
Carpet and Floor Covering

There are few additions you can make to the interior of your home that can make so great a difference in its appearance as floor covering. The visual impact of new carpeting, vinyl flooring, or wood flooring is far beyond the cost of the flooring. Some dealers of decorating products have decorating consultants who are trained to help you make your decorating decisions. If you can't afford to replace all your floor coverings every time a new color fad comes into vogue, ask the dealer to help you choose a more traditional color or pattern that will not go out of favor before the carpet is worn out.

As with most building materials we advise to buy the very best floor coverings you can afford. The goal with floor covering is to buy materials that will retain that "new look" and will present a good appearance over the long term with a minimum of maintenance. The key is quality.

CARPET

Because carpet replacement represents a major investment, you should take the time to read and understand the carpet label and warranty information. The first step is to be sure the carpet was made by a major manufacturer, and that the carpet warranty will be honored. Next, check the type of yarn used (wool, nylon, or polyester) and the number of stitches per square inch of carpet.

Both the type of yarn used and the density (stitches per square inch) are important in considering the quality and durability of the carpet. Using fine, small fibers yields more stitches per square inch, or greater density. Fold the carpet sample in half or spread the pile apart with your fingers and visually inspect the carpet construction: more stitches per inch mean better quality and longer wear.

Check the carpet style—Berber, Saxony, or Frieze, for example—and the qualities of each style.

The weight, shown in ounces per square yard, is also an important indication of carpet quality. Check too whether the yarn was pre-dyed, meaning the color is continuous through the yarn, or whether the carpet was first manufactured, then solution-dyed. Pre-dyed carpet will clean better and hold its color better than solution-dyed carpet.

Type of Yarn

Wool is the most expensive type of carpet yarn. Wool carpets combine appearance, luxury, natural stain resistance, and durability.

For a good carpet at less-than-wool prices, look for one that is 100 percent nylon fiber. Beware of polyester or polyester/nylon fiber blends. These may have good initial appearance, at bargain prices, but polyester carpets fall short in such attributes as durability, tendency toward matting, and ease of cleaning.

Berber carpets with olefin fibers are commercial grade with high durability. The Berbers have tight loop construction so dirt cannot penetrate, and they wear like iron. Consider a Berber where traffic volume is high: Berbers won't show wear patterns in living rooms, recreation areas, hallways, or other high-traffic areas.

Carpet Styles

In addition to the Berber carpets, look for Saxony or plush styles. Saxony carpets have dense, wound fibers that are practically "trackless" or non-directional. These carpets are ideal anywhere in the home. Frieze carpets can be turned any direction for laying because they have no grain pattern, and they wear well without showing tracking.

Carpet Pads

Beware of "bargain" bait-and-switch ads for carpeting. Although labor costs vary by region, you should figure labor costs for installing carpet at between $3 and $5 per square yard, and a good pad will cost at least $3 per yard. If you figure that you'll pay between $6 and $8 for pad and installation, obviously a package "bargain" of $10 per yard for carpet, pad, and installation is suspect.

A common tactic is to sell you one pad and install another, cheaper pad. And the pad quality is as important, or more important than, the carpet quality.

Select a carpet pad that is between 6 and 8 pounds per square yard density. Polypropylene or rebond pads that are made from multicolor (usually red and blue) plastic chips are a good choice both for quality and cost. The minimum pad weight for low-traffic areas such as bedrooms should be no less than 4½ pounds, with 6-pound weight preferred for better resiliency and carpet wear.

Avoid "prime" or polyurethane pads that are a single color and formed in a single sheet rather than bonded chips. This type of plastic foam tends to lose its resiliency and "bottom out." Without the cushion of a good pad the carpet will suffer impact wear and damage from being pounded between the floor and passing feet.

The best pad is solid rubber, which may have a guarantee of thirty years or more. A solid rubber pad of 6 to 8 pounds per yard will literally last forever, so you can replace the carpet many times without buying a new pad. If you intend to keep your home for years, the rubber pad is a good long-term investment.

Many people spend their money on the carpet and buy a cheap pad. According to carpet installers, you should actually do the reverse: invest in a good pad and a medium-grade carpet. A compromise of pad and carpet might be to buy a 6 to 8 pound per yard rebond pad and a 40-ounce carpet.

If you select a heavier carpet, something with a weight of 60 to 70 ounces per yard, have the installer bid for a second visit to restretch the carpet. Heavy carpets are stiff and hard to stretch: if you leave it in place for a couple of months you can often take up extra slack and pull the carpet tight. Loose carpets will wrinkle, and your feet will drag along the top edges or peaks of the wrinkles. This will cause premature wear, and you'll soon be vacuuming up your investment.

Installing pad and carpeting is not a do-it-yourself task. Stretching, making seams, and laying carpet require both special tools and special training. It is possible, however, to lay padded or foamback ("kangaback") carpet yourself and save the installation costs.

When laying padded or foamback carpet, be sure that you buy enough carpet to do the job. Round up your measurement to the next full footage number, ignoring any odd inches.

If you are installing the foamback carpet in a basement, over concrete floors, you should first seal the concrete and let it dry. To avoid having the new carpet smell in the house, unroll the carpet outside, on a deck or patio, and let it air out before bringing the carpet indoors. When the carpet has aired out for a day or two, reroll the carpet and take it into the room where you will install it.

Remove any base shoe and molding. Roll out the carpet and let it lie loose for at least twenty-four hours so it will lose any wrinkles and lie smooth. Position the carpet so any overlap folds up the wall.

You can secure foamback carpet in place using carpet adhesive. Buy the adhesive recommended by your carpet supplier and use a notched trowel spreader to spread the adhesive over the floor. The best technique is to fold back one half of the carpet, apply adhesive to the exposed floor area, then position the glued end of the carpet. Then fold the unglued end of the carpet back, spread the adhesive, and position the remaining carpet over the adhesive.

Use a sharp razor knife to cut the excess carpet away and fit the carpet edge to the wall. Or you may be able to rent or borrow a carpet-cutting tool that is designed to fold the carpet at the wall and cut it for a proper fit. Be very careful if cutting with a razor knife, because it is easy to miscut with an ordinary knife. Remember that base molding and/or base shoe will cover any narrow gaps between the carpet and the walls.

For laying carpet in small areas, you can use double-faced carpet tape (tape that has an adhesive on both sides) to hold the edges in place. Lay the carpet out and let it "relax" or lose any wrinkles. Be sure you have cleaned the floor surface carefully, because any dirt or lint will interfere with getting a good grip with the adhesive tape.

Making Carpet Last

How can you keep your carpet investment looking its best, and get all the life the carpet was designed to deliver? Here is a list of tips for caring for carpet:

- Install a quality pad under the carpet.

- Place large door mats at all entry doors. Most dirt in your house is tracked in on your shoes.

- Keep house shoes or slippers handy and remove your shoes at the door. Mister Rogers, who always removes his street shoes when he comes inside, is a good example for us all.

- Buy a vacuum sweeper that has a "beater bar" to lift dirt out of the carpet fibers for complete removal.

- Vacuum the carpet frequently, even daily for high traffic areas or for large families. Grit that is allowed to penetrate into the base of the carpet will cut the fibers and shorten the life of even a quality carpet.

- Don't walk barefoot on carpets. Wear slippers. Oil secretions from human skin pick up and hold dirt, making a dirty track down your carpet.

- Buy stainless carpet and wipe up any spills immediately. A good trick to remove spilled liquids is to cover the spill with layers of paper toweling and then step on the towels to force the liquid out of the fiber.

- Need a carpet cleaner that will remove almost any stain from carpet? Our installer swears by a cleaning product called TECH, available at many hardware and home center stores.

VINYL FLOOR COVERING

As with carpet buying, the key to buying quality sheet goods or vinyl floor coverings is to read and understand the product specifications as shown on the product label and in the product's descriptive literature. Common vinyl floor covering that is offered as a special or price leader, selling in the price range of from $10 to $15 per square yard, most often has a very thin wear layer (surface) that is only 10 to 15 mils (mils are thousandths of an inch) in thickness. By comparison, a tough, quality floor covering that will stand up to constant foot traffic will have a wear layer that is 25 to 35 mils thick.

Although the surface of the lightweight 10-15 mil wear layer may look good on the showroom floor or in the sample book, it does not take much wear and abuse to damage or destroy such a thin wear layer. Most people are forced by their budgets to live with the shoddy quality if they are misled into buying it. The key is closer examination of the product, and buying the floor covering as an investment.

Cheaper vinyl floor coverings are rotogravure or printed patterns, covered with a thin, 10-15 mil clear wear surface. If you see a floor covering sample that has a knobby texture on the face, it is a rotogravure pattern. The knobby finish is caused by rollers, or by a bonding machine, that press the primary layer and the top or wear layers together. The resulting knobby surface is hard to clean and maintain, because dirt will collect in the tiny valleys, so it will be hard to lift out and wash away.

For a quality floor covering that will wear well and look terrific after years of abuse, buy an inlaid vinyl. *Inlaid* means the design particles are dropped onto the base material, then covered with the wear layer, rather than being a printed pattern like the rotogravure. A quality inlaid vinyl such as Mannington Gold or Armstrong Solarian may have a wear layer that is 25 to 30 mils thick.

What do you pay for quality in vinyl floor covering? Remember the rule when buying quality: labor for installing cheap materials costs the same as for installing quality materials. All you can save is the cost difference between the materials. The cheap 10 mil rotogravure will cost $15 per square yard, and the quality inlaid goods will cost about twice as much, or $30 per square yard. For a 12' x 18' kitchen floor of 24 square yards, the rotogravure will cost $360, the inlaid $720. How large an item is $360, after all, in the kitchen facelift budget? The pro installers are sure you will be happier, and save money in the long run, with the better quality floor.

Installation

Some of the vinyl floor coverings are offered as do-it-yourself materials, but installing sheet goods can be a difficult way for the amateur to save money. If you buy a thicker, inlaid product, it will be stiff and hard to lay. Only the thinner rotogravure material is flexible enough to be easily handled by the amateur. We suggest that you ask your dealer to suggest an installer and have the material professionally laid.

Whether or not you can install your new floor covering over the existing floor covering is a difficult question to answer. If you are having an inexpensive rotogravure installed, the old material pattern may photograph through the new material. Removing the old floor covering and adhesives is a difficult job, plus the fact that older materials may contain asbestos. In many or most cases the installer will suggest that he should install an underlayment of ¼-inch lauan plywood on top of the existing floor, leaving the old floor covering in place. This is a judgment call, and depends on a number of factors, including whether existing door clearances will permit the added thickness of the ¼-inch plywood plus the ⅛-inch thickness of the vinyl floor covering. Because there are variable factors that demand a judgment call, you should rely on the judgment of the installer, especially so if you propose to ask the installer to guarantee the work.

Vinyl Tile

Vinyl floor tile can be purchased either "dry back," meaning adhesives must be applied to the surface to be tiled, or "adhesive back," which has the adhesive or peel-and-stick back. Although we prefer a vinyl floor that is made from sheet goods, easy one-person installation and peel-and-stick convenience make vinyl tile a viable flooring option for some areas. Vinyl floor tile are often used by do-it-yourselfers in such areas as recreation and hobby rooms, and in finished basement or attic expansion projects.

Directions for estimating how much vinyl tile you will need are often printed on the side of the tile carton. Buy and use the tile adhesive recommended by the manufacturer, if you will be installing dry back tile. Also included in each carton of tile is an instruction sheet telling you how to apply that particular tile.

Consider the surface over which you will apply the floor tile. If the surface to be tiled is new plywood sheathing, you should use a product such as Durham's Rock Hard Water Putty to smooth and fill all joints and nail heads in the sheathing. This will ensure that uneven joints or hammer dimples around nail heads will not photograph through the finished floor tile. In addition to the Durham's or other floor filler, you will need a mixing container,

a paint stick for stirring and mixing the wood filler, and a trowel or wide putty knife to spread the wood filler. Other tools you will need include a notched adhesive spreading trowel if you are installing dry back tile, a measuring tape, and a sharp razor knife and straight edge for cutting the tile. Also, use a chalk line to establish the mid-point of the room to be tiled. All tile application jobs begin at the center of the room, to ensure that you have uniform border tiles at the edges of the finished floor, as well as a clean, professional-looking, and well-done installation.

Keep in mind that tiles that are solid colors are easy to lay. Tiles that have a pattern or design must be laid in the proper direction so that the design is continuous and not interrupted. There may be arrows on the back of any patterned tile to help you maintain the pattern direction throughout the entire project.

To ensure uniformity of color from tile to tile check to be sure the tile cartons you buy all have the same lot numbers. Also, some tile directions recommend that you open several cartons of tile and alternate using tile from different cartons to be sure there is no obvious and abrupt color change or shift from one carton to another.

WOOD FLOORING

A generation of yuppies who grew up playing on the carpeted floors popular in the '60s and '70s have rediscovered hardwood floors. Wood floors have been for centuries both a comfortable and attractive flooring materials option. If you check out the floors in one of our historic mansions you may find wood floors that have lasted for 200 years or more and have grown more beautiful with each passing decade. For example, at President Jackson's home, the Hermitage, just north of Nashville, Tennessee, the tulipwood floors are more than 160 years old, and they witness the passing of thousands of feet each year; yet the passing has only made the floors more attractive.

Today a wide array of pre-finished hardwood flooring choices is offered to the consumer. Wood flooring is available either in tongue-and-groove planks or in parquet style, and in a variety of wood species and finishes. Most of these can be installed by the do-it-yourselfer, and can be either nailed or glued in place—projects that are within the abilities of the average d-i-y'er.

Prior to the availability of pre-finished wood flooring products, one had to sand, fill, seal, and finish bare wood. Sanding and finishing were far more difficult tasks than installing the flooring. The factory-applied floor finishes let the applicator "nail on the finish" and avoid the on-site problems associated with wood finishing. Modern wood finishes provide a durable walking surface and also make the wood floors easy to maintain.

Our advice, if you want the look of wood floors, is to install real wood, rather than the simulated-but-don't-look-like-real-wood finishes you will find on vinyl or vinyl tile. The house-buying public today is moving toward quality and use of authentic materials, and is bypassing the faux or artificial finishes.

Read the manufacturer's literature for advice on how to maintain your new wood floors. Most experts agree that the most important thing you can do for your floors is to keep door mats in place at entry doors. Most of the dirt and grit that damage your floors is tracked into the house on your shoes, so remove street shoes at the door.

Most of the flooring products today can be maintained with a daily application of the electric broom, and a weekly wet-mopping. Some manufacturers recommend using a paste floor wax as added protection from damage by grit and dirt. Read and heed the maintenance instructions that are supplied with your new flooring, and respect the floor care advice and expertise of the manufacturer.

ALTERNATIVE FLOORING

The flooring products discussed above are the most popular and affordable flooring options for the homeowner. There are other flooring materials options, mostly found in the higher price brackets and requiring pro level skills for installation. These flooring materials include ceramic or quarry tile, marble, terrazzo, slate, and flagstone.

These quality flooring options can represent a sizable cash investment, but the investment is one that can be recovered if it is made in an upper-bracket house. And most of these quality flooring options, unlike their less expensive cousins, not only will last for decades, they will improve in appearance as they age.

Maintenance is also greatly reduced when you use natural and durable flooring products. Most of these hard-surface floors require only an occasional cleaning with an electric broom, a monthly damp mopping, and an annual coat of sealer. This is not a hard and fast rule, of course: the amount of maintenance time required will depend on the material you choose and the amount of traffic that passes over the floor.

For example, I once grew weary with the upkeep required on a cheap sheet vinyl floor. The floor got heavy traffic in a family with two parents and four teenagers, and it required a constant routine of cleaning, waxing, removing the wax, and rewaxing. This was a get-on-your-knees-and-scrub area that encompassed both a family-sized kitchen and an adjoining formal dining room floor.

To solve the maintenance problem I installed a flagstone (also referred to as a crab orchard flagstone) floor. The flagstone materials dealer told me to follow the above maintenance procedure—vacuum when dirty, damp-mop monthly, and apply a floor sealer once a year. As the years passed the flagstone took on a depth and beauty that cannot be achieved using manmade flooring materials.

Should you consider one of these more expensive flooring options? The quality vinyl floor coverings (and carpeting and wood) are now used and buyer-accepted even in homes in upper price brackets. But the natural flooring choices, such as slate, marble, and flagstone, still have that look of class and permanence, and you should certainly, at the least, get price comparisons on these floors before you make your buying decision.

13.
Products that Solve Problems

When I was a staff editor for a home magazine I received many telephone calls and letters from readers who needed help with a home repair problem. Most often they did not know which product might solve their problem. Throughout this book we have tried to offer helpful advice to guide you in making a choice between products that are included in the same category. We have also suggested some specific products that may help solve any particular problem you might have. In this chapter we'll do a roundup that will help you find just the product you need to successfully complete your do-it-yourself project.

Before we get down to talking about specific problems, here's some advice on how and where to find any product. Even if your dealer does not handle or stock a particular product, he can special order it for you, or tell you how to contact the manufacturer and order the product direct for yourself. If you know the name of the product's manufacturer, you can always look up the address and/or the telephone number in the AT&T 800-number directory or in the Directory of Advertisers. Both are available at your local library.

PLASTER CRACKS

PROBLEM: Plaster cracks most often are structural cracks, meaning they are caused by expansion and contraction of the plaster or of the studs or joists to which the plaster is attached. Because these materials move with each change in temperature or humidity, using a brittle patching material such as patch plaster or any patching product will not effect a permanent cure. The next time the material moves the patch will crack again. There is always a stress point in the wall or ceiling plaster, usually at corners of the room or corners of openings such as windows and doors. The cracks will occur at these stress points, and that is where they will open up again when the material moves.

CURE: At some plaster crack locations the movement is so severe that making a permanent patch will be impossible. But most cracks can be patched if you first reinforce the crack. To do this, clean loose plaster out of the crack, then fill the crack with wallboard taping compound. Let the prefill compound dry, then tape the crack just as you would tape the joint in wallboard. Do not use adhesive-backed fiberglass tape to patch cracks. Use regular paper wallboard tape. Wipe away the excess taping compound and then cover the tape with a very thin coat of taping compound. This thin fill coat is needed to cover the edges of the tape so they will not be visible through the paint. Let this first fill coat dry. Then apply a second thin or "shear" coat of taping compound, using a shearing motion to wipe the compound over the tape, then shear all the excess compound away. Let the compound set until it is firm but not dry, then use a damp sponge or a Wallboard Wet Sander to smooth the compound. Prime and paint the repair area when the compound is completely dry.

HOLES IN PLASTER

PROBLEM: If one or more plaster coats fails because of water damage or impact damage, or simply due to age, you can refill the plaster hole with patch plaster. The plaster will be kept in place if the base lath is still intact. However, the new patch material may fail to bond with the old plaster, and a crack will occur around the edge of the patch. This is caused in part by the old plaster and lath soaking up the water from the patching plaster, causing excessive shrinkage and cracking of the patch material.

CURE: To avoid this problem and prevent failure of the patching material, buy the latex bonding adhesive sold as a concrete bonder. This patching adhesive can be used to bond concrete, plaster, or stucco repairs. One such product, and there are many, is Concrete Bonding Adhesive, made by Quikrete. To apply the product, first clean the repair area to remove any loose plaster, dirt, or grease. Then use a paint brush to coat the edges of the old plaster, and the lath base, with the bonding adhesive. Some bonding products suggest that you mix the patching compound with the bonding adhesive as well. Follow label directions for using your particular bonding product.

PEELING PAINT

PROBLEM: Peeling exterior paint may be caused by a buildup of many layers or coats of paint, so that the paint film is too thick. To avoid this, let the old paint film age and become thin before repainting: too frequent painting causes the paint buildup and peeling. Peeling paint may also be caused by painting over a dirty surface.

CURE: Use a wood deck cleaning product, such as DEKSWOOD by the Flood Co., or Wood Renew by Darworth, to clean the house siding, trim, soffits, or porch ceilings. Use a stiff scrub brush to apply the cleaner. After applying the wood-cleaning product use a power washer to blast all old dirt and chalked paint from the surface. It is especially important to clean any areas that are protected and not washed by rain. This includes the underside of roof overhangs or soffits and the ceilings of any porches. Paint that is not washed by the rain will not wear down and clean properly.

PROBLEM: Paint often peels on the trim around windows and doors. This happens because interior moisture is trying to escape to the outside in cold weather, and the moisture will pass through the wood trim and peel the exterior paint. Moisture often escapes through the window and door trim because there is no vapor barrier at these points or because any vapor barrier has been interrupted by the openings.

CURE: To reduce or stop peeling on trim paint, first sand or scrape away all loose paint. Then apply a coat of Penetrol (use with alkyd or oil paints only) to the peeled area. Next, mix alkyd or oil trim paints 50/50 with Penetrol. Finally, apply a finish coat of the oil-base paint. If your dealer does not stock Penetrol, ask him to order it or call the Flood Co., in Hudson, OH, at (800) 321-3444.

PROBLEM: Paint peeling on siding, on the gable ends of a house (where the peeling is not occurring on the rest of the siding), is caused by too little ventilation in the house attic. Attic moisture is penetrating through the back (unpainted) surface of the siding and is trapped when it reaches the exterior paint film, so it lifts and peels the paint.

CURE: To stop paint from peeling on the siding on gable ends, install extra ventilators. These vents can be louvered gable vents, or an upgraded vent system featuring continuous venting along both the soffits and the roof ridge, or it can be done with a power vent. (The last is the least favorite choice: ventilation should occur naturally, without being forced.) If you solve your attic ventilation problem, you will end the paint peeling problem on your gable ends.

CLEANING/PAINTING ALUMINUM SIDING

PROBLEM: If you bought "lifetime" aluminum siding, you may be dismayed to learn that all paint, even the finish on aluminum siding, will fade and fail in time. Many owners of houses with aluminum siding lack an understanding of the options open when the paint finish on their siding fails.

CURE: If the paint film on aluminum siding is intact and only faded or chalked, you can use one of the deck-cleaning products to clean the siding. One product that we've used is DEKSWOOD by the Flood Co. This cleaner contains oxalic acid, which is a bleach product. Mix the concentrated cleaner with water, following label directions. You can apply the cleaner with a clean cloth or large sponge, scrubbing the chalked paint away, then rinse (before the cleaned area dries) with clear water. If the cleaned siding has a good appearance, no further action is necessary.

If the siding finish is clean but dull, you can clear-coat the siding to bring back the sheen of the finish. Use Penetrol, made by the Flood Co. (see above for a phone number) applied with clean cloths, as the clear coating finish. Change the cloths frequently to avoid spreading dirt back onto the paint surface. You can buy cleaning cloths or painters' rags by the pound at paint stores that cater to professional painters. Penetrol will renew the sheen of the siding paint and will provide a good base for future painting when you decide that is necessary.

If you decide to repaint the aluminum siding, you can do so with your favorite acrylic latex house paint. Read the product label to be sure your paint is recommended for use on aluminum. Pittsburgh Paint, for example, offers latex house paints in colors to match the original paint colors from the aluminum siding manufacturers, or you may choose to paint the house any new color.

STAINS ON PAINT

PROBLEM: While in the contracting business I often was faced with trying to paint over walls or ceilings that had various hard-to-cover stains. These difficult stains may be water stains from leaking roofs or plumbing; rust stains from leaking water or steam heating pipes; oil or grease cooking stains in the kitchen; children's crayon art on walls; or smoke and grease stains from a house fire. If you try to apply latex paint over any of these stains the staining material may be activated by the water in the paint and often will bleed through the new finish.

CURE: The first step is to remove the staining material or as much of it as possible. Trisodium phosphate or TSP is a dry powder that can be mixed in whatever strength or concentration is necessary to remove the staining material. If you are concerned about the phosphates (and we all should be), Savogran now makes a phosphate-free TSP cleaner. TSP will remove most soiling agents, including much or most of the smoke from fire-damaged walls or ceilings.

For stains that cannot be removed with TSP, check your home center for products such as Goof Off!, a high-strength stain remover that will remove lipstick, crayon, oil, or magic marker stains. If one of these cleaners will remove all the staining material, you can then paint as usual without any further action.

If all the staining material cannot be removed, use a shellac sealer such as BIN to cover the stain and seal it so it cannot be activated by the paint. I have found BIN to be very useful in covering such stains as rust on a ceiling, caused by a leaking steam radiator on the floor above, and for sealing smoke-damaged walls that were covered with an oily film from the house fire. BIN is also an excellent base coat for use under any high gloss enamel. High gloss finishes will lose part of their sheen if they are applied over a surface that is not completely sealed.

CLEANING PAINTING TOOLS

PROBLEM: With the growing emphasis on concern for the environment, there has been a national movement towards using more environmentally friendly products. Oil-base paints are increasingly yielding to latex or water-base paints because the latex paints are less polluting. One of the advantages of latex paints is soap and water cleanup: we no longer have to buy chemical solvents to thin paint or to clean up our painting tools when we use water-base latex paints. But no matter how well we clean our paint brushes or rollers, it seems that there is enough paint residue to cause the tools to be stiff and hard when we use them again. Brush and roller cleaning solutions will help clean out the latex paint residue, but using these products does not solve our environmental concerns. And disposable brushes and rollers also add to the waste stream.

CURE: Buy a $10 tool called the Brush & Roller Cleaner. The tool is made by SHUR-LINE Mfg. Company of Lancaster, PA. The tool is a tubular device with a handle and a spiral drive shaft on one end, and a claw end that is shaped to hold either a paint brush or roller. As one works the handle up and down the claw end spins, using the same technique as a child's toy top. As the attached tool—paint brush or roller—spins rapidly, it flings any residual paint out of the tool, using centrifugal force. Paint brushes or rollers cleaned in this way will always be soft and ready for use the next time you need them.

SANDING

PROBLEM: When I have sanding to do, my years of experience in using abrasives professionally always steers me toward 3M sanding products. I have used a lot of sandpaper on sanding blocks and on power sanders, and I've found 3M products to be non-clogging and long-lasting. If you have to do sanding take precautions: wear protective goggles and an approved dust mask to avoid injury from the sanding dust. But there are ways to avoid sanding and the dust mess that goes with it.

CURE: There are ways to avoid sanding when doing the usual home maintenance chores. For smoothing plaster or wallboard repairs, buy a Wallboard Wet Sander, a sponge device that has an abrasive face attached. The wet sander is made by the Padco Co. Wet sanding eliminates both health hazards and cleanup from sanding dust.

Use a wet sander for major wallboard projects as well as for smoothing repairs. Many people who try the wet sander become frustrated with it, because wet sanding is not as fast as sanding with sandpaper. The trick is to keep the wet sander handy as you work, and keep an eye on any finished area as it dries. When the repair material is firm, but not completely dry, you can begin wet sanding. The patch plaster or wallboard compound must be firm enough that the wet sander will not smear it and ruin your repair, but still soft enough that it can be smoothed without excessive effort or waiting. If you wait until the job is completely dry, wet sanding is a slow and painful process.

Liquid Sanders

For painting trim, interior wood molding, and cabinetry, you must use sandpaper to smooth the edges of any nicks or chipped areas in the paint. But to degloss the old paint finish and to remove any grease or wax from the surface to prepare it for painting, you need not use sandpaper. Instead, use a liquid sander product such as No Sand by Klean-Strip. To use this liquid sander, saturate a clean cloth with the product and wipe the surface to be painted thoroughly. It is important to observe the time frame noted on the product label: Apply liquid sander only to the area that can be painted within thirty minutes, or according to label directions. As with any chemical, you should use liquid sander with adequate ventilation and observe label precautions.

CONCRETE PROBLEMS

PROBLEM: Suppose you have concrete steps, a sidewalk, or a garage floor that has started to sag or tilt out of level. In the past the only solution was to break out the old concrete, dispose of the debris, and repour your concrete structure. Today, in most cities there are other, less expensive alternatives.

CURE: This is not a product cure but a pro solution for a difficult and expensive problem. In most cities large enough to have concrete-in-transit trucks you can have professionals jack up and level your concrete steps or slabs. The correctional procedure is to drill holes in the concrete surface, insert a material hose, and pump a concrete slurry into the hole. The concrete slurry will spread beneath the concrete structure and raise it back into its original position. For professional help, look in the phone book Yellow Pages under "Concrete Contractors." The service may be described as "Raising," "Lifting," or "Mudjacking" of concrete.

RENEWING FIBERGLASS

PROBLEM: If you have vinyl siding or a fiberglass boat or motor home that looks faded, the bids for repainting may be high. Still, the vinyl or fiberglass may look so dingy that it is unattractive.

CURE: Follow the directions above for cleaning and renewing aluminum siding. The DEKS-WOOD cleaner by Flood Co. can be used to clean vinyl siding and fiberglass objects as well as aluminum, and the Penetrol product can be used to clear-coat the material and bring back the gloss to the finish.

Fiberglass Tubs and Showers

PROBLEM: When it was first introduced to the building market, fiberglass plumbing ware became very popular as an economical and no-maintenance option to the ceramic tiled bath and shower areas. But tubs and showers of fiberglass are formed under high pressure, and the forms leave small pores in the fiberglass product. These tiny pores can trap and hold soap scum and minerals from hard water. Once stained, the fiberglass tub or shower may be impossible to clean.

CURE: Wax the sides or walls of shower stalls with paste automotive wax, but don't wax the floor, to avoid slipping and injury in the tub or shower. The wax will help avoid buildup of soap or hard water residues on the fixture. Wipe the fixture down with your bath towel after you've dried yourself off, to avoid water spotting and staining.

Another option is to clean and seal any fiberglass product with Gel Gloss. Gel Gloss will clean the fiberglass (boat, RV, tub, or shower) and leave a high luster that is easy to wipe clean. Just reapply the product when the surface begins to lose its luster or is hard to wipe clean. Gel Gloss is widely available in home centers or super markets, and is made by TR Industries in Lynwood, CA.

REMOVING OLD LINOLEUM

PROBLEM: A typical problem for remodelers is how to remove existing linoleum or other sheet floor covering from kitchen and bath floors. It is a very difficult task to remove the old floor covering and the adhesive to clean the subfloor so new floor covering can be laid atop it.

CURE: The first option is to hire a pro to remove the old floor covering. Pros use a power tool that has a blade with a horizontal scissors action. This horizontal cutting bar is placed underneath the edge of the old floor covering and the back-and-forth action cuts the old floor covering free from the floor underlayment.

Another option is to use an electric heat gun to soften the adhesive so the old floor covering can be pried up with a scraper. This is definitely a difficult and time-consuming solution.

The best solution is to remove the base shoe, leave the old floor covering in place, and nail a new underlayment of ³/₈-inch lauan plywood over the old floor covering. This is a particularly desirable solution if the old floor covering may contain asbestos, which is better left in place than disturbed. Use a product such as Durham's Rock Hard Water Putty to smooth and level the joints between the plywood sheets and to fill the nail holes.

REMOVING ADHESIVE

PROBLEM: Many people choose to remove floor covering or plastic wall tile, then are faced with the problem of removing the old adhesive from the walls or floors. As stated, our best advice is to cover the old floor covering with a new underlayment plywood, rather than removing it. But if you must remove old adhesive from a wall or floor, there are a couple of tips that will make it easier.

CURE: For cleaning away old adhesive, the first tool you will need is a wallpaper scraper with a razor-type cutting blade (this blade is both wider and stronger than the familiar blade in the razor knife). Red Devil makes one such tool. Unlike the edge on a putty knife or paint scraper, this sharp razor-type blade will cut underneath the adhesive coating and lift it. To soften the adhesive for easier removal, buy Tile Pro Adhesive Remover, made by Midland Chicago Corp. of Alsip, IL 60658. The Adhesive Remover is a useful product for cleaning adhesive from tools or from tile when you are doing an installation, and also can be used to help remove old adhesives.

REMOVING WALL COVERINGS

PROBLEM: One frustrating decorating task is removing old wall coverings, either paper or vinyl. Many of the newer wall coverings are strippable, meaning to remove them you need only lift a corner of a sheet and pull it away. You can use a sponge and hot water to remove the remaining residue. The residue may be wall covering adhesive only, or it may be a peel-away base layer of paper. But older wall coverings were applied with a generous coating of adhesives and were sometimes applied in multiple layers. Removing these wall coverings can be a frustrating task, but there are both techniques and materials that will make the job go easier.

CURE: To begin, keep in mind that the entire problem of removing wall covering is to get enough moisture underneath the covering to soften the adhesive.

If the adhesive is softened, the coverings will literally fall off the walls, so any steps you take that will help promote moisture penetration through the coverings will aid in removal. Tools you'll need to ease wall covering removal include a device called a "Paper Tiger" from Red Devil. Other similar tools are available. The tool has a serrated edge that will puncture coated or vinyl wall coverings to let moisture penetrate down to the adhesive and soften it. Next, you will need wall covering removal tools: use a paper remover with a razor blade if you are removing the wall coverings from a hard plastered surface, or use a paint scraper or broad knife if the covered surface is softer wallboard. You will also need a large sponge or sponge mop to apply the hot water and a paper remover solution, such as Savogran's FAST Wallpaper Remover. This type of concentrated remover product can be added to hot water to speed softening of the adhesive.

Techniques that are helpful include: wet down a large area of wall covering, even an entire room (depending on the temperature and humidity level on the day you are doing the work). Don't peck away at small areas: you need a lot of soak time to let the water and remover solution attack and soften the wall covering adhesive. You can place a humidifier in the work area to help maintain humidity levels and give the remover time to work. After waiting at least ten minutes for the remover to work, test a spot of wall covering with your wide blade scraper. If the wall covering peels away easily, proceed with the removal. If the adhesive is still hard, soak and wait. Don't chip away at the wall covering, and don't be in a hurry. If you give the water and remover time to work, the wall covering will come off easily.

Appendices

1. Helpful Math and Formulas

2. Manufacturers' Toll-Free Numbers

1.
Helpful Math and Formulas

CONVERTING ENGLISH TO METRIC

Inches x 25.4 = millimeters

Feet x .3048 = meters

Miles x 1.6093 = kilometers

Square inches x 6.4515 = square centimeters

Square feet x .09290 = square meters

Cubic inches x 16.3872 = cubic centimeters

Cubic feet x .02832 = cubic meters

Cubic yards x .76452 = cubic meters

Ounces x 28.35 = grams

Pounds x .4536 = kilograms

Tons (2,000 lbs.) x .9072 = metric tons

Horsepower x .746 = kilowatts

CONVERTING METRIC TO ENGLISH

Millimeters x .03937 = inches

Meters x 3.2809 = feet

Kilometers x .62138 = miles

Square centimeters x .155 = square inches

Square meters x 10.7641 = square feet

Cubic centimeters x .06103 = cubic inches

Cubic meters x 35.314 = cubic feet

Cubic meters x 1.308 = cubic yards

Grams x .03527 = ounces

Kilograms x 2.2046 = pounds

Metric tons x 1.1023 = tons (2,000 pounds)

Kilowatts x 1.3405 = horsepower

LAYING OUT A SQUARE CORNER

When building a deck or any square structure you can make a square corner by using the carpenter's "3-4-5" method, otherwise known as the Pythagorean Theorem. First, drive a wooden corner stake, then tie two lengths of mason's string to the corner stake. Measure out on either string a distance of 3 feet, and mark the string at that point. Then measure out 4 feet on the other string, and mark the string at that point. Now move the two strings apart until the distance between the marks on the two strings is 5 feet. Drive stakes to hold the two lines in this position. The corner thus created is square. How do we know? Because Pythagoras stated that, in a right triangle (one with a 90° or square corner) the square of the hypotenuse is equal to the sum of the squares of the other two sides: 3 x 3 + 4 x 4 = 5 x 5, or 9 + 16 = 25. This is the easy way to lay out a square corner when you have no other reference point.

FOOTING DEPTHS

To avoid frost heave under foundations, the depth of footings must be below the frostline; i.e., the depth at which the ground freezes in your area. So how deep should the footings (or posts) be set to avoid frost heaves, in the area where you live? Here is a guide:

- If it never freezes the soil in your area, build footings 1'6" (18") deep.

- If the coldest winter temperature in your area is 20° F, dig posts or footings 2'6" deep.

- For each further 10° drop in winter temperature, dig posts or footings down another 6 inches:

20° F: 2'6"

10° F: 3'0"

0° F: 3'6"

-10° F: 4'0"

-20° F: 4'6"

HEADER SPANS

So you're installing a new window, and you need a wider opening. How should you build a new header to support the load above? The first step is to double up the 2x material, with a ½-inch thick piece of plywood as a spacer between the 2x's. The size lumber to use for a given span is:

Lumber size	Span
2 x 4	3'0"
2 x 6	5'0"
2 x 8	7'0"
2 x 10	8'0"
2 x 12	9'0"

MATH FORMULAS

Circumference of a circle = pi (3.1416) x diameter

Diameter of a circle = circumference x .31831

Area of a circle = pi x radius squared

Area of a square = length x width

Area of a rectangle = length x width

Area of a triangle = ½ base x height

Volume of a cube = length x width x height

Volume of a sphere = diameter cubed x .5236 or dia x dia x dia x .5236

Volume of a cylinder = pi (3.1416) x radius squared x height

Double the diameter of a pipe = quadruple the capacity

1 gallon of water = 8½ pounds = 231 cu. inches

7½ gallons of water = 62½ pounds = 1 cu. ft.

CUBIC MEASURE

1,728 cu. inches = 1 cubic foot

27 cu. feet = 1 cubic yard

SAND, CONCRETE, ETC.

1 cubic foot sand = 100 pounds

1 cubic yard sand = 2,700 pounds

1 ton = 3/4 yard, 20 cu. ft.

1 shovel = 15 pounds

NOTE: An easy-to-remember concrete formula is: 1-2-3, or 1 part Portland cement + 2 parts sand + 3 parts gravel = concrete.

Formula for mortar for block, brick, or stone: 1 part masonry cement to 2-3 parts sand.

Concrete and mortar mix ingredients should be dry mixed, with water added last, and sparingly. The reason for this is that one cannot estimate the amount of water that is contained in bulk sand.

ESTIMATING MATERIALS

Estimating materials can be a chancy business because of a number of variables we will try to explain. The best way to figure materials is to measure the area to be covered and take the figures to the dealer for pro help in estimating. We will try to give you some useful pointers, but we would caution you to heed professional advice, not to follow your own judgment. A common mistake is to measure short in the name of economy and then run short and have to make a special trip to buy extra materials. In addition to having to make an extra trip, your new material may have a different lot number from the original material, so colors may not be an exact match. This is especially common when buying wall covering, floor tile, or carpet.

The other tip to keep in mind is always to buy enough materials so you can save leftovers for use in future repairs. Almost all material colors go out of favor, and you may not be able to buy the same color material if repairs are necessary in the future. A common example of this color problem occurs with ceramic tile. Buy enough material to do the job. In most cases the dealer will let you return unopened containers or cases of material: ask for dealer confirmation of return privileges before you buy the product. Some materials, such as custom-mixed paint colors, are not accepted in return, so try to figure your needs within a gallon. Keep in mind, however, that you should always buy and save extra material for future repairs.

Carpet

A very good example of bad estimating can be made in figuring carpet requirements. Homeowners tend to figure room dimensions to the inch, then try to calculate the required yardage to the bare minimum to save money. The result can be that, depending on the way the nap runs, the carpet remnant cannot be turned and still match the rest of the floor, because the reversed nap may change the hue or color of the carpet. Or the size of the room may be such that a lot of waste is created that cannot be used without making a patchwork of the job. For example, carpet (and vinyl floor covering) comes in rolls that are 12 feet wide. If the carpet is laid in a room that is 11 feet wide, you will have a leftover strip of carpet that is 1 foot wide and as long as the room. This is waste that can rarely be used if the job is to be done in a workmanlike manner. Buying minimum yardage may mean that the installer has to make unnecessary seams in the carpet to use up all the scraps. Seams in carpet may be hard to conceal and may show premature wear. For the price of a couple of yards of carpet you can avoid the problem. Use leftover scraps of carpet for area rugs, or for door mats, or save them so you have material in case of needed repair.

Wallboard

Estimating for wallboard is a fairly easy job. For small jobs, simply measure the area to be covered in square feet and divide by either 32 sq. ft. (for 4' x 8' sheets) or 48 (for 4' x 12' sheets). If you have large openings in the walls (a sliding patio door or picture windows), you can subtract that measurement in square feet from the total. For most openings, you should simply estimate the wallboard on a "solid wall" basis, i.e., figure the area to be covered as though there were no openings. This is true because most cutout pieces of wallboard—those cut out for openings—are waste. One big mistake people make is to try to use up every last scrap of wallboard. Wallboard is one of the cheapest of building materials, and you can afford to throw the waste away. But more important, a quality wallboard job is based on the fact that you will plan joint placement so there are as few joints as possible. The whole idea is to conceal any joints, so why would one make a patchwork of the job, with many unnecessary joints, simply to save a few pieces of scrap? Remember: the goal is to cover the area while creating as few joints as possible: the goal is not to see how few sheets of material you can get away with. It has always amazed me to see people try to use up all their wallboard scrap in a closet, for example. The wallboard costs only a few dollars per sheet: you will waste countless hours cutting and fitting all those little scraps into a closet, then you will waste many more hours trying to tape and finish all those joints. How many hours are you willing to waste to save $5, the cost of one sheet of wallboard?

Estimating wallboard for ceilings only is easy to do. If you multiply the length x the width of the room, and round the total up so it is divisible by either 32 sq. ft. (the 4' x 8' sheet) or by 48 sq. ft. (the 4' x 12' sheet), you will arrive at the number of sheets needed. But lay the area out on graph paper: de-

pending on the measurements of the room and how the sheets will fit, you may have to order an extra sheet or two of wallboard, to avoid fitting in all the scrap and ending up with a multitude of small, hard-to-finish joints.

If you are estimating the wallboard for an entire new house, you can multiply the floor space in square feet by 3½, and get a close estimate of the total amount of wallboard needed to cover all the walls and ceilings in the entire house. For example: Let us assume a 3-bedroom house with a total of 1,500 sq. ft. of floor space. If we multiply the floor space or 1,500 sq. ft. x 3½ we get 5,250 sq. ft. of wallboard. This is a ballpark figure, and cannot be exact unless we know how open the floor plan is. Obviously, an open floor plan where there are few or no interior walls between the kitchen, dining room, and living room, and lots of windows and glass space, will require somewhat less than 5,200 sq. ft. of wallboard. If we chop the same floor space into tiny rooms, all walled in, the extra walls may bring the total wallboard needed up to 5,500 sq. ft., or even more. But the formula is a good working formula for estimating wallboard for an entire house, if you remember that it is just an estimate.

Paint

For any paint, interior or exterior, the recommended spread rate on the label is usually about 400 sq. ft. per gallon, when recoating. This is true whether you are painting exterior (smooth) siding or interior plaster or wallboard. Although it is often possible to roll paint out with a roller, covering perhaps as much as 600 sq. ft. per gallon, it is important to note here that you should try to apply the paint at the rate recommended by the manufacturer. Meeting the intended application or spread rate is critical for proper coverage or "hide" over old paint colors, and to get a paint film thickness that will stand up to future washing. One can hardly blame the manufacturer if the paint doesn't cover old colors, or if it scrubs off with the first washing, if you make the paint coat thinner than suggested.

Especially if you are having colors custom-mixed, it is important to have enough paint to finish the entire job, or at least enough to finish one entire side of the house (if painting the exterior) or to paint an entire room (if painting on the interior). The problem is that slight color variations may result in mixing. If you stop painting in mid-wall, then begin with a new can of paint, you may get a color shift that will be very noticeable. Try to estimate the job so that you buy enough paint before starting the job.

If you are estimating the amount of area to be painted, measure the length x the height of the walls. Next, measure and subtract out any doors or large windows. If you will be painting the trim around the base, doors, and windows with the same paint you are using for the walls, do not subtract the footage of the room openings, because it will take about the same amount of paint to paint the trim and/or window frame and doors as it would take to paint solid walls with no openings.

Trim paint is less critical. Because it is applied over a smaller area or a series of areas such as multiple windows, you will not notice a color shift from one area to the next. Try to estimate the paint needed as closely as possible, but you can always return for another quart if needed.

An exciting development that is becoming increasingly available is a color computer that will let you plug in a photo of your own house and use computer colorization to see how it would look in any given color. It is difficult for many of us to visualize a color sample on an entire house: color selection by computer lets you see the house in the color you're considering before you actually paint the house.

Computer Estimating

In increasing numbers, home centers are installing computers that can not only help you design a project such as a deck, they will print out a materials list when you have settled on your design. It may be helpful for you to rough out a design on graph paper, and try to estimate material needs before getting down to shopping. But an experienced dealer can not only figure the materials list more accurately, he can save you materials—and money —on your project.

Here is an example of how a knowledgeable person can help you reduce the cost of a deck. Let us say that you plan a simple 12' x 12' deck. If you design the deck to use 24-inch joist spacing, or plan to set the joists 24 inches o.c., you will have to use 2 x 4 or 2 x 6 lumber for deck boards. However, by setting the joists 16 inches o.c. you can save money—and lumber—by using 1 x 6 deck boards rather than 2-inch (nominal) thick deck boards. Then, if you build in perimeter seating or benches on the deck, these benches can serve both as a guard railing and as deck furniture, again saving you money. Take all the free help you can get, to build better and to save money on materials.

How-to Videotapes

Another good idea is to rent or buy how-to videotapes and view them before you begin either planning a project or shopping for materials. These how-to tapes will advise you on what type of fasteners to use (galvanized or stainless steel screws and/or nails for decks, for example) and will also give advice on estimating materials, plus handy tips for solving any problems you encounter. Increasingly, home centers and lumber yards are stocking how-to tapes and other materials, such as books and informational brochures, to help their customers do maintenance and remodeling projects.

2.
Manufacturers' Toll-free Numbers

A large number of manufacturers in the home products field have 800-numbers to provide toll-free advice and/or information to consumers. Check the manufacturer's labels on the products you buy to find whether they have an 800-number listing. These numbers can be a very handy and valuable source of information and advice for the do-it-yourselfer.

Following is a partial listing of 800-numbers, listing manufacturers of home repair products. The list is not complete. You can also check the consumer's 800-directory from AT&T, or the complete directory of 800-numbers at your local library. Some of these 800-numbers are intended for use by businesses only, others are intended as an information source for consumer use. Again, check labels and product brochure and warranty information for individual company 800-numbers. It is also useful to jot down the addresses and phone numbers of manufacturers of your favorite home repair products, keeping your own phone book for future reference.

APPLIANCES

AMANA
(800) 843-0304

FRIGIDAIRE
(800) 451-7007

GE, HOTPOINT, RCA
(800) 626-2000

KELVINATOR
(800) 323-7773

KITCHENAID
(800) 422-1230

WHIRLPOOL
(800) 253-1301

WHITE-WESTINGHOUSE
(800) 245-0600

CAULK AND WEATHERSTRIPPING

DAP INC.
(800) 543-3840

GE
(800) 255-8886

GEOCEL
(800) 348-7615

MACKLANBURG-DUNCAN
(800) 654-8454

FIREPLACES

HEATILATOR
(800) 728-2650

WYNDHAM FIREPLACE CO.
(800) 225-4765

FLOORING

KENTUCKY WOOD FLOORS
(800) 235-5235

MANNINGTON RESIDENTIAL FLOORS
(800) 356-6787

NATIONAL WOOD FLOORING ASSN.
(800) 848-8824

GARDEN POWER EQUIPMENT

GARDEN WAY
(800) 828-5500

HOFFCO
(800) 999-8161

HONDA
(800) 426-7701

JCPENNEY
(800) 222-6161

LAWN BOY
(800) 526-6937

MANTIS
(800) 366-6268

HEAT GUNS

BLACK & DECKER
(800) 762-6672

MILWAUKEE
(800) 558-8880

WAGNER
(800) 328-8251

LOCKS

BRINKS HOME SECURITY
(800) 347-5247

WEISER LOCK
(800) 558-8700

LUMBER

TRUSJOIST CORP.
(800) 338-0515

WEYERHAUSER
(800) 548-5767

MASKING PRODUCTS

DAUBERT COATED PRODUCTS
(800) 634-1303

METAL CONNECTORS

KANT SAG
(800) KANT-SAG

LUMBERLOK
(800) 221-7905
In California: (800) 221-7906

TECO
(800) GET-TECO

PAINT

DARWORTH CO.
(800) 624-7767

DEVOE
(800) 654-2616

DUTCH BOY
(800) 828-5669

FLECTO CO.
(800) 6FLECTO

FORMBY'S
(800) FORMBYS

FULLER O'BRIEN
(800) 368-2068

LIVOS PLANT CHEMISTRY
(800) 621-2591

LUCITE
(800) 426-3606

PITTSBURGH PAINT
(800) 441-9695

PLASTI-KOTE
(800) 431-5928

PRATT & LAMBERT
(800) 922-2272

SEARS
(800) 972-4687

TRU-TEST
(800) 922-0061

UGL
(800) UGL-LABS

PAINT REMOVERS

BIX
(800) 251-1098

PARKS
(800) 225-8543

SAVOGRAN
(800) 225-9872

3M
(800) 842-4946

PLUMBING WARE

AMERICAN STANDARD
(800) 821-7700

BEAUTY WARE
(800) 521-3244

MOEN
(800) 347-6636

ROOFING

OWENS CORNING FIBERGLAS
(800) ROOF-OCF

PABCO ROOFING PRODUCTS
(800) 776-3563

STEPLADDERS

ARCHBOLD
(800) 537-0531

LYNN
(800) 523-5463

WHITE METAL
(800) 321-3415

STONE, MASONRY

LATICRETE INT'L
(800) 243-4788

STUCCO STONE
(800) 225-1727
IN CALIFORNIA: (800) 445-9877

UGL
(800) UGL-LABS

Z-BRICK
(800) 828-0253

THERMOSTATS

HONEYWELL CONTROLS
(800) 468-1502 EXT. 3302

ROBERTSHAW
(800) 421-1130
IN CALIFORNIA: (800) 262-1173

TOOLS

Power Tools

PORTER CABLE
(800) 321-9443

RYOBI
(800) 525-2579

WEN
(800) 462-3630

Hand Tools

GOLDBLATT
(800) 255-4099

STARRETT
(800) 772-3649

WINDOWS

ANDERSEN CORP.
(800) 426-4261

MARVIN WINDOWS
(800) 346-5128

PEASE INDUSTRIES
(800) 543-1180

POZZI WOOD WINDOWS
(800) 821-1016

ROTO FRANK OF AMERICA INC.
(800) 243-0893

WEATHER SHIELD
(800) 477-6808

MISCELLANEOUS

ALCOA BLDG. PRODUCTS
(800) 962-6973

CARRIER CORP.
(800) CARRIER
Air Conditioning

CHENEY
(800) 782-1222
Home Elevators

CLAIRSON INT'L
(800) 221-0641
Storage

CLOPAY
(800) 225-6729
Garage Doors

FORMICA CORP.
(800) 524-0159

FROHOCK-STEWART
(800) 343-6059
Bath Access Aids

M&S SYSTEMS
(800) 877-6631
Home Safes

MERCER PRODUCTS
(800) 447-8442
Rubber Flooring

MOULTRIE MFG.
(800) 841-8674
Moldings, Trim

NUTONE
(800) 543-8687
Lighting, Chimes, Exhaust Fans

Index